ACOUSTIC GUITAR
PRIVATE LESSONS

Explore
ALTERNATE TUNINGS

In-depth lessons for players of all levels

by the Master Teachers at *Acoustic Guitar* magazine

and AcousticGuitar.com

STRING
LETTER

Publisher: David A. Lusterman

Group Publisher and Editorial Director: Dan Gabel

Editor: Jeffrey Pepper Rodgers

Music Editor and Engraver: Andrew DuBrock

Production Manager: Hugh O'Connor

Art Director: Barbara Summer

Design and Production: Kristin Wallace

© 2011 Stringletter

ISBN 978-1-936604-02-9

This book was produced by Stringletter, Inc.

PO Box 767, San Anselmo, CA 94979-0767

(415) 485-6946; StringLetter.com

Library of Congress Cataloging-in-Publication Data

Explore alternate tunings : in-depth lessons for players of all levels / by the master teachers at
Acoustic guitar magazine ; [Jeffrey Pepper Rodgers, David Hodge, Mark Hanson, ... [et al.]].
    p. cm. -- (Acoustic guitar private lessons)
  Includes bibliographical references and index.
  ISBN 978-1-936604-02-9 (alk. paper)
  1. Guitar--Instruction and study. 2. Guitar--Tuning. I. Rodgers, Jeffrey Pepper, 1964- II.
Hodge, David, 1957- III. Hanson, Mark, 1951- IV. Acoustic guitar.
    MT580.E96 2011
    787.87'1928--dc22
                  2011015020

CONTENTS

INTRODUCTION 4

MUSIC NOTATION KEY 5

GET STARTED

CD Track No.

1   **DROPPED-D TUNING** Jeffrey Pepper Rodgers 8
9   *Dropping D Blues* 11

10   **DROPPING THE THIRD STRING** David Hodge 12
17   *Handsome Molly* 16

18   **ACCOMPANIMENT IN OPEN G AND OPEN D** Mark Hanson 18

37   **INTRO TO D A D G A D** Doug Young 26
43   *Down by the Salley Gardens* 30

MOVE ON

44   **EXPLORE D A D G A D** Doug Young 32
51   *Whiskey Before Breakfast* 35
58   *Octave Blues* 40

60   **HAWAIIAN SLACK-KEY GUITAR** Fran Guidry 42
68   *Salomila* 44

69   **C G D G B E TUNING** Sean McGowan 46
75   *Fanny Poer* 50

76   **ORKNEY TUNING** Steve Baughman 52
86   *The Almost Whisky Waltz* 56

87   **HIGH-STRUNG TUNING** Doug Young 57
93   *John Barleycorn* 60

BONUS SONGS

94   **PRELUDE FROM THE CELLO SUITE NO. 1 IN G MAJOR** Patrick Francis . . . 62

96   **OLD JOE CLARK** Joe Miller 66

98   **HI'ILAWE** Patrick Landeza 68

ABOUT THE TEACHERS 70

INTRODUCTION

The simple act of changing the tuning of your guitar—even just one string—has a magical effect: it's almost as if you have a new instrument. All kinds of sounds become available that you couldn't play in standard tuning—deep bass notes, evocative jazzy chords achieved with one or two fingers, new melodic patterns . . . Familiar fingerings produce strange and surprising results, sparking new song and arrangement ideas.

The flip side of all this novelty is that at least some of what you know how to play no longer applies—you have to reorient yourself on the fingerboard because the notes have shifted around. So alternate tunings are both alluring and disorienting, and a little bit of guidance makes a big difference. In these lessons the master teachers at *Acoustic Guitar* help you get oriented in an array of alternate tunings used in many styles of contemporary music. Think of it as a travel guide for your own explorations of alternate tunings.

The first section introduces ways to get started by retuning only one string, and then proceeds with the

popular open G, open D, and D A D G A D tunings. The second section digs deeper into D A D G A D as well as tunings used in Hawaiian slack-key guitar, Celtic music, and Nashville studio sessions. You'll find songs to play throughout, plus three bonus songs to round out this book: the slack-key classic "Hi'ilawe," the old-time favorite "Old Joe Clark," and a beautiful arrangement of a prelude from Bach's cello suite.

Happy exploring!

—*Jeffrey Pepper Rodgers*

MUSIC NOTATION KEY

The music in this book is written in standard notation and tablature. Here's how to read it.

Standard Notation

Standard notation is written on a five-line staff. Notes are written in alphabetical order from A to G.

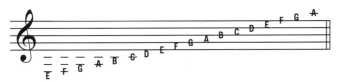

The duration of a note is determined by three things: the note head, stem, and flag. A whole note (o) equals four beats. A half note (♩) is half of that: two beats. A quarter note (♩) equals one beat, an eighth note (♪) equals half of one beat, and a 16th note (♬) is a quarter beat (there are four 16th notes per beat).

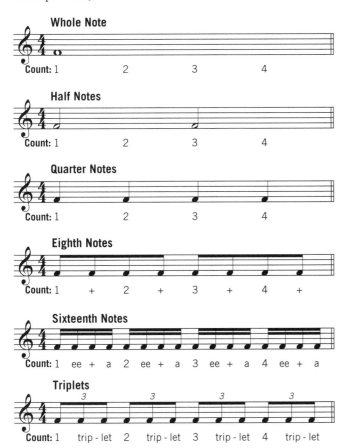

The fraction (4/4, 3/4, 6/8, etc.) or ℂ character shown at the beginning of a piece of music denotes the time signature. The top number tells you how many beats are in each measure, and the bottom number indicates the rhythmic value of each beat (4 equals a quarter note, 8 equals an eighth note, 16 equals a 16th note, and 2 equals a half note). The most common time signature is 4/4, which signifies four quarter notes per measure and is sometimes designated with the symbol ℂ (for common time). The symbol ¢ stands for cut time (2/2). Most songs are either in 4/4 or 3/4.

Tablature

In tablature, the six horizontal lines represent the six strings of the guitar, with the first string on the top and sixth on the bottom. The numbers refer to fret numbers on a given string. The notation and tablature in this book are designed to be used in tandem—refer to the notation to get the rhythmic information and note durations, and refer to the tablature to get the exact locations of the notes on the guitar fingerboard.

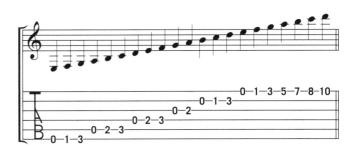

Fingerings

Fingerings are indicated with small numbers and letters in the notation. Fretting-hand fingering is indicated with 1 for the index finger, 2 the middle, 3 the ring, 4 the pinky, and *T* the thumb. Picking-hand fingering is indicated by *i* for the index finger, *m* the middle, *a* the ring, *c* the pinky, and *p* the thumb. Circled numbers indicate the string the note is played on. Remember that the fingerings indicated are only suggestions; if you find a different way that works better for you, use it.

Pick and Strum Direction

In music played with a flatpick, downstrokes (toward the floor) and upstrokes (toward the ceiling) are shown as follows. Slashes in the notation and tablature indicate a strum through the previously played chord.

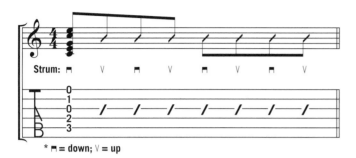

* ⊓ = down; V = up

Chord Diagrams

Chord diagrams show where the fingers go on the fingerboard. Frets are shown horizontally. The thick top line represents the nut. A fret number to the right of a diagram indicates a chord played higher up the neck (in this case the top horizontal line is thin). Strings are shown as vertical lines. The line on the far left represents the sixth (lowest) string, and the line on the far right represents the first (highest) string. Dots show where the fingers go, and thick horizontal lines indicate barres. Numbers above the diagram are left-hand finger numbers, as used in standard notation. Again, the fingerings are only suggestions. An *X* indicates a string that should be muted or not played; 0 indicates an open string.

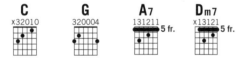

Capos

If a capo is used, a Roman numeral indicates the fret where the capo should be placed. The standard notation and tablature is written as if the capo were the nut of the guitar. For instance, a tune capoed anywhere up the neck and played using key-of-G chord shapes and fingerings will be written in the key of G. Likewise, open strings held down by the capo are written as open strings.

Tunings

Alternate guitar tunings are given from the lowest (sixth) string to the highest (first) string. For instance, D A D G B E indicates standard tuning with the bottom string dropped to D. Standard notation for songs in alternate tunings always reflects the actual pitches of the notes. Arrows underneath tuning notes indicate strings that are altered from standard tuning and whether they are tuned up or down.

Vocal Tunes

Vocal tunes are sometimes written with a fully tabbed-out introduction and a vocal melody with chord diagrams for the rest of the piece. The tab intro is usually your indication of which strum or fingerpicking pattern to use in the rest of the piece. The melody with lyrics underneath is the melody sung by the vocalist. Occasionally, smaller notes are written with the melody to indicate the harmony part sung by another vocalist. These are not to be confused with cue notes, which are small notes that indicate melodies that vary when a section is repeated. Listen to a recording of the piece to get a feel for the guitar accompaniment and to hear the singing if you aren't skilled at reading vocal melodies.

Articulations

There are a number of ways you can articulate a note on the guitar. Notes connected with slurs (not to be confused with ties) in the tablature or standard notation are articulated with either a hammer-on, pull-off, or slide. Lower notes slurred to higher notes are played as hammer-ons; higher notes slurred to lower notes are played as pull-offs. While it's usually obvious that slurred notes are played as hammer-ons or pull-offs, an *H* or *P* is included above the tablature as an extra reminder.

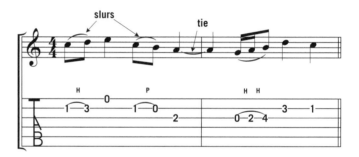

Slides are represented with a dash, and an *S* is included above the tab. A dash preceding a note represents a slide into the note from an indefinite point in the direction of the slide; a dash following a note indicates a slide off of the note to an indefinite point in the direction of the slide. For two slurred notes connected with a slide, you should pick the first note and then slide into the second.

Bends are represented with upward curves, as shown in the next example. Most bends have a specific destination pitch—the number above the bend symbol shows how much the bend raises the string's pitch: ¼ for a slight bend, ½ for a half step, 1 for a whole step.

6

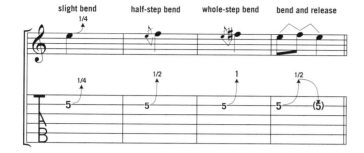

Repeats

One of the most confusing parts of a musical score can be the navigation symbols, such as repeats, *D.S. al Coda*, *D.C. al Fine*, *To Coda*, etc. Repeat symbols are placed at the beginning and end of the passage to be repeated.

Grace notes are represented by small notes with a dash through the stem in standard notation and with small numbers in the tab. A grace note is a very quick ornament leading into a note, most commonly executed as a hammer-on, pull-off, or slide. In the first example below, pluck the note at the fifth fret on the beat, then quickly hammer onto the seventh fret. The second example is executed as a quick pull-off from the second fret to the open string. In the third example, both notes at the fifth fret are played simultaneously (even though it appears that the fifth fret, fourth string, is to be played by itself), then the seventh fret, fourth string, is quickly hammered.

You should ignore repeat symbols with the dots on the right side the first time you encounter them; when you come to a repeat symbol with dots on the left side, jump back to the previous repeat symbol facing the opposite direction (if there is no previous symbol, go to the beginning of the piece). The next time you come to the repeat symbol, ignore it and keep going unless it includes instructions such as "Repeat three times."

A section will often have a different ending after each repeat. The example below includes a first and a second ending. Play until you hit the repeat symbol, jump back to the previous repeat symbol and play until you reach the bracketed first ending, skip the measures under the bracket and jump immediately to the second ending, and then continue.

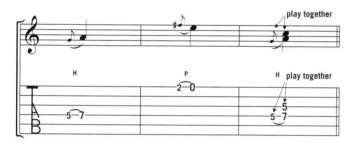

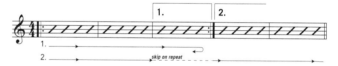

D.S. stands for *dal segno* or "from the sign." When you encounter this indication, jump immediately to the sign (𝄋). *D.S.* is usually accompanied by *al Fine* or *al Coda*. *Fine* indicates the end of a piece. A coda is a final passage near the end of a piece and is indicated with ⊕. *D.S. al Coda* simply tells you to jump back to the sign and continue on until you are instructed to jump to the coda, indicated with *To Coda* ⊕.

Harmonics

Harmonics are represented by diamond-shaped notes in the standard notation and a small dot next to the tablature numbers. Natural harmonics are indicated with the text "Harmonics" or "Harm." above the tablature. Harmonics articulated with the right hand (often called artificial harmonics) include the text "R.H. Harmonics" or "R.H. Harm." above the tab. Right-hand harmonics are executed by lightly touching the harmonic node (usually 12 frets above the open string or fretted note) with the right-hand index finger and plucking the string with the thumb or ring finger or pick. For extended phrases played with right-hand harmonics, the fretted notes are shown in the tab along with instructions to touch the harmonics 12 frets above the notes.

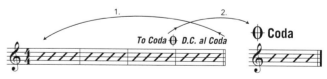

D.C. stands for *da capo* or "from the beginning." Jump to the top of the piece when you encounter this indication.

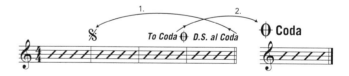

D.C. al Fine tells you to jump to the beginning of a tune and continue until you encounter the *Fine* indicating the end of the piece (ignore the *Fine* the first time through).

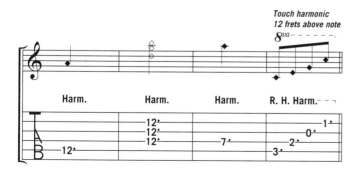

DROPPED-D TUNING

Jeffrey Pepper Rodgers

Pick up your guitar and strum an open E or G chord—listen to that nice, full sound, from the deep bass note up to those ringing treble strings. Now play a standard D, with its root on the fourth string and the fifth and sixth strings left out. Sounds a little wimpy by comparison, doesn't it? Don't you wish you could play all the strings on the D chord and hear a stronger bass note underneath it all?

Well, your wish can come true, thanks to the magic of dropped-D tuning, where you lower the sixth string to D and leave the other strings alone. Dropped D does more than just allow you to play a big-sounding D chord; it opens up all sorts of enticing new possibilities while allowing you to use most of your hard-won knowledge of chords and notes on the fingerboard—after all, five of the six strings haven't changed. Dabble in dropped D and you'll quickly see why it's used by guitarists all over the stylistic map, from folk to rock, blues to bluegrass, Celtic to classical (see "Classic Songs in Dropped D" for inspiration). After decades of playing, I find that my own guitar increasingly lives in dropped D for all sorts of original tunes and arrangements, delicate fingerstyle pieces and hard-driving flatpicked songs alike. Beware: dropped-D tuning is addicting.

Tune Down

To get into dropped D, just lower your sixth string a whole step (the equivalent of two frets) to D. Use **Example 1** to check the pitch. First match the sixth string, seventh fret, against the open fifth string. Then check the open sixth string against the open fourth string; they are now an octave apart. Finally, if you play the open sixth, fifth, and fourth strings (as in measure 3), you have D–A–D—instant power chord!

Now that you're in tune, check out the first measure of **Example 2**: these are the D major and D minor chords you already know, but in dropped D you can strum all six strings for a sound that's every bit as big as an E or G. (No one will dare kick sand in the face of *this* D chord!)

Dropped D, of course, requires some adjustments to the standard fingerings: you have to play any notes on the sixth string *two frets higher* to compensate for the lower tuning. That's why the bass note of the G chords in measure 2 is up at the fifth fret. The G5 voicing leaves out the first string (and instead of fretting the fifth string, you could mute it by resting your ring finger against it). Next comes Em and Em7, where you hold down the sixth string at the second fret to get an E in

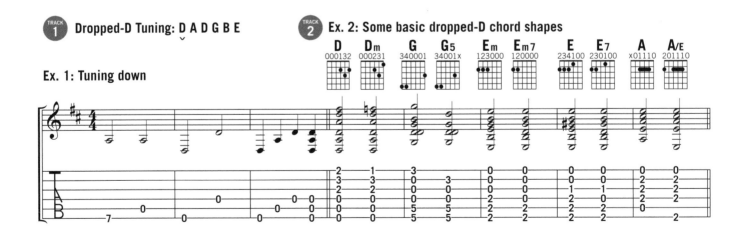

Ex. 1: Tuning down

Ex. 2: Some basic dropped-D chord shapes

the bass. You can play the Em with either three fingers or (my preference) an index-finger barre. E major is a bit awkward, with four fingers scrunched together; E7 is more comfortable.

You can play a standard A chord on the top five strings, but if you want to add a low E to the bass, you need to hold down the second fret of the sixth string, as in measure 5 of Example 2. I play the A with an index-finger barre, so my middle finger is free to fret the sixth string. You may find a different fingering more comfortable: for instance, you could use your ring finger for the barre and grab the bass note with the middle finger, or use your index for the bass and the other fingers to form the A shape. If this position is too much of a finger buster, just stick with your usual A form and steer clear of the sixth string.

How about your old nemesis, the F chord? Dropped D allows you to play the friendly, full-sounding F in **Example 3**. This voicing is also movable—slide it up two frets for a G. Lean your ring finger (which is fretting the sixth string) against the fifth string to

mute it. This example shows a little progression that leads to a D chord spiffed up with a James Taylor–esque hammer-on.

Drop and Groove

Let's put these chords to work in some more short progressions. Take them slowly and loop them until the changes flow smoothly. **Example 4** is an arpeggio idea that takes advantage of the low D string with an ascending bass line over D, G, and A chords. **Example 5** is a hymnlike passage that kicks off with a nice alternative voicing for a D chord—the F♯ has moved from its usual spot on top to the fourth string, making a rich-sounding chord with plenty of low-end punch. In **Example 6**, notice the old faithful C chord—since this fingering doesn't use the sixth string, we can play it in the usual fashion. **Example 7** moves from Dm to Am with a couple of simple embellishments. Keep your fingers in the Dm shape throughout the first measure, but lift your index finger off the first string to grab the open-string notes near the end of the bar.

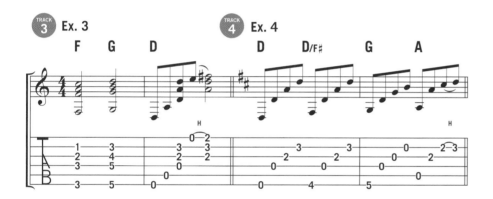

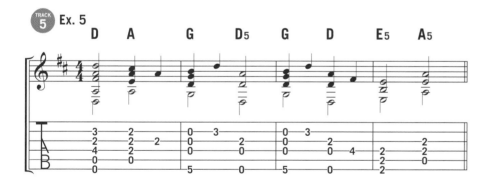

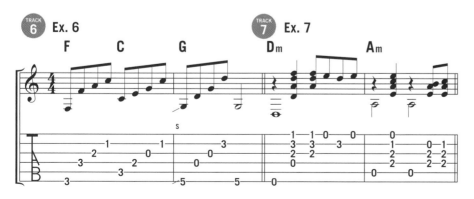

> Tune down that sixth string to extend your bass range while still preserving your hard-earned knowledge of standard tuning.

One of my favorite uses of dropped-D tuning is with blues and roots-rock grooves. Dropped D works so well in this context in part because of the D–A–D power chord on the bottom three strings, and also because the "blue notes" of the scale are so easy to grab. In a D blues scale, the blue notes are C (the flatted-seventh of D) and F (the flatted-third), both of which are conveniently and symmetrically located at the third fret on the sixth, fifth, and fourth strings in dropped D. In **Example 8**, hold down a D position with your index and ring finger (leaving out the first string), even when you're not playing those upper strings, and play the scale notes on the low strings with your middle finger. While you're playing, give the third-fret notes a slight pull toward the floor with your fretting fingers to accentuate their bluesiness. Slight bends like this are much easier on the bass strings than on the treble strings.

Drop Some Blues

Let's play around with these ideas in a ditty called "Dropping D Blues." This tune is built around the D, G, and A fingerings you've already played and makes liberal use of the blue notes from Example 8. I've added a bass-line intro in measure 1, and in measure 7 I throw in an F chord as a transition between G and D. Don't worry too much about hitting the exact strings indicated in the tab. As long as you're holding down the right chord position, you can add or subtract notes freely. The groove is the important thing. Listen to the CD to get the hang of it.

Classic Songs in Dropped D

"Fishing Blues," Henry Thomas
(famously covered by Taj Mahal)
"Blackwaterside," Bert Jansch
"Embryonic Journey," Jorma Kaukonen
"Dear Prudence," the Beatles
"Wondering Where the Lions Are," Bruce Cockburn
"Harvest Moon," Neil Young
"Grace," Jeff Buckley
"Country Road," James Taylor
"Living in the Country," Pete Seeger

TRACK 8 **Ex. 8**
D5

Dropping D Blues

Music by Jeffrey Pepper Rodgers

 Played up to Speed

Dropped-D Tuning: D A D G B E

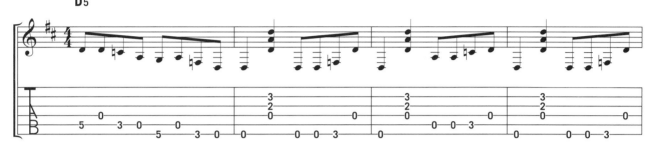

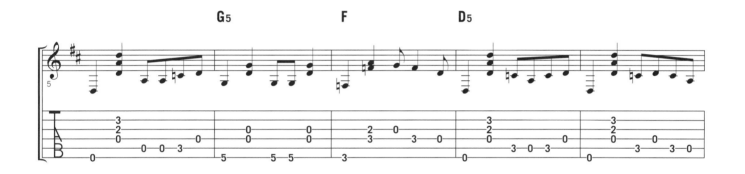

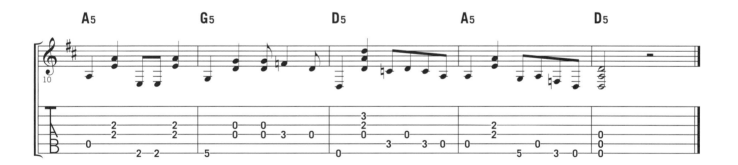

DROPPING THE THIRD STRING

David Hodge

When beginners find out there is more than one way to tune the guitar, their reaction is usually something like, "You mean I just learned all these chords and now I have to relearn everything?" An understandable response, of course. But exploring different chords and chord voicings can help you find new approaches to songwriting and arranging, and trying an alternate tuning, which immediately makes you search for new chords, is a good way to start thinking and experimenting. And that's always a good thing. In this lesson I'll take a very simple, yet unusual, alternate tuning and show you how to find chords and begin to navigate around in it. And then, to put what you've learned to use, I'll show you a simple arrangement of the traditional song "Handsome Molly."

The most common alternate tuning is probably dropped D, where you just lower the low E (sixth) string to D. In this lesson we'll try something a little more challenging that still changes only one string: the tuning E A D F♯ B E, where the third string is tuned down but all the others stay in standard tuning. A lot of old classical guitar pieces (many originally written for lute) use this tuning, and I think you'll find it a great way to continue your alternate tuning adventures.

Tune Down

To go from standard tuning to E A D F♯ B E, just lower your third string a half step from G to F♯. If you don't have a chromatic tuner, match the sound of the third string to the fourth

fret of the D string instead of the fifth fret, as you usually would.

Now let's go exploring. First, we'll see what basic chords are available. Strike the open strings one by one and listen to what you've done. Can you hear the D-major chord you get when you play the fifth (A), fourth (D), and third strings (F♯)? How about the B-minor chord with the fourth (D), third (F♯), and second (B) strings? As you may know, in standard tuning the interval between strings is a fourth, except for the interval between the third (G) and second (B) strings, which is a major third. In E A D F♯ B E, that major third interval has been shifted down to the fourth (D) and third (F♯) strings. Consequently, you're going to be in for a pleasant surprise when you start figuring out chords in this tuning.

That Chord Looks Familiar

Let's look at some first-position fingerings for chords commonly found in the keys of E and E minor. Each chord uses a shape that should be familiar.

See how each E chord in **Example 1** has exactly the same shape as its A chord counterpart in standard tuning, but on different strings? The E major is the same as A major, but fingered on the third, fourth, and fifth strings instead of the second, third, and fourth. Likewise Em, E7, and Em7 are the same shapes as the standard-tuning Am, A7, and Am7 shapes, just moved over a string.

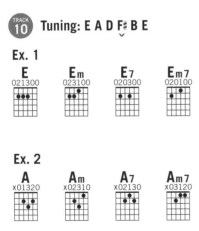

TRACK 10 Tuning: E A D F♯ B E

Ex. 1

E	Em	E7	Em7
021300	023100	020300	020100

Ex. 2

A	Am	A7	Am7
x01320	x02310	x02130	x03120

Notice that each of the A chords in this new tuning, as shown in **Example 2**, is exactly the same shape as its corresponding D chord in standard tuning, again with each finger on the next lower string. So you've just learned eight chords of a new tuning!

The B chord fingerings in **Example 3** are totally new, but aren't the B and Bm a lot easier than the barre chords you have to deal with in standard tuning? The seventh chords are a little work at first, but with some practice they will become second nature.

As in standard tuning, chords vary in difficulty. **Example 4** shows a sampling of other open-position chords to try. Some, such as D and Dm, are pretty easy, since they use shapes you probably already know (use an Am shape for the D; simply slide the index finger down one fret for the Dm), while others, like G, C, and F, are the same as their standard tuning counterparts, but with one note added or, in the case of F, altered.

New Sounds

These more difficult chords give us the opportunity to find some interesting and beautiful chord voicings by working with the new tuning instead of against it. For example, if you leave the third string open when you finger the new G shape in Example 3, you get a very nice Gmaj7 chord that would be

very difficult to play in standard tuning. And if you leave the high string (E) open as well, you might come up with something like the arpeggio pattern in the first measure of **Example 5**. If you leave the second string open in the new C shape and add a low G bass note, you'll get the Cmaj7/G of the second measure. It's easier to look at the fingering of this chord as an open-position Bm chord (XX4432) that has been moved to a new home on your fretboard. The third measure starts with the Am7 you learned from Example 2, followed by a really simple fingering of D9. Who knew ninth chords could be so easy to play?

This is why it's important to noodle around in any alternate tuning you try. Who knows what you'll find? I experimented with some hammer-ons and pull-offs while playing

Ex. 3

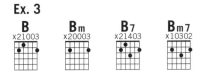

Ex. 4

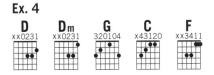

Ex. 5

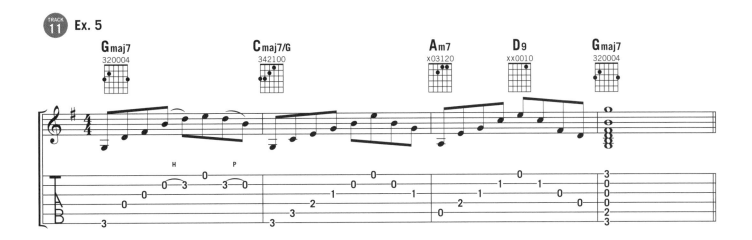

an E-major chord and came up with the rhythm pattern in **Example 6**. Try it yourself; it's as easy as placing two fingers on the fretboard. In standard tuning, you'd never be able to get the sound of hammering-on from F♯ to G♯ on the third string. G to G♯, while simple enough, is sometimes too bluesy. Getting the double-hammer of the A to B on the fifth string is a pleasant bonus, and it didn't take me long to be totally taken with this sound. So let's see where we can go from here.

It turns out you can do a similar thing with the A chord, as in **Example 7**. If you try the fingering of the E chord shown

in **Example 8**, with your index finger on the second fret of the D string, you can swing between the E and A chords by hammering and pulling off with your middle and ring fingers. It flows wonderfully, and it sounds great either with straight strumming or in almost any kind of fingerpicking pattern, such as those in Example 8 and **Example 9**.

We've got a good thing going with the E and A chords, which in the key of E are the I and IV chords. Since most traditional folk, blues, and just about all rock 'n' roll songs use the V chord, let's come up with something simple for a B

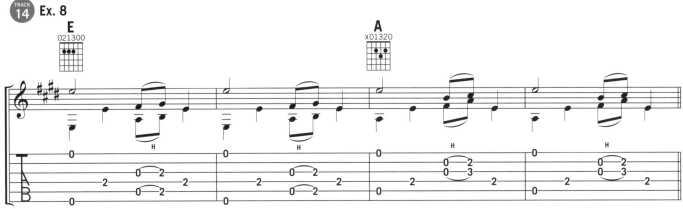

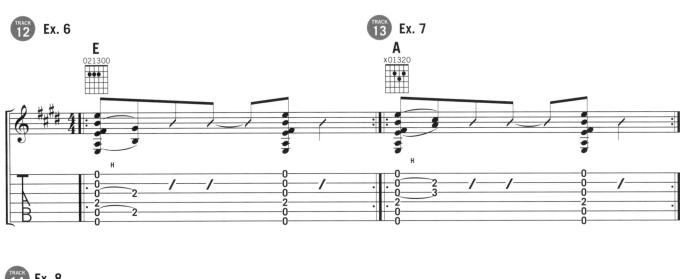

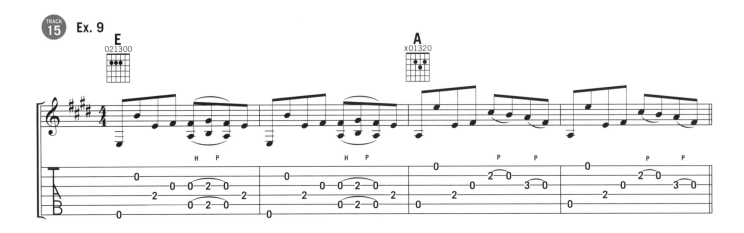

chord, which is the V in the key of E. Use your ring finger to pull off and hammer onto the second fret of the first two strings, as in **Example 10**. This certainly qualifies as easy and it blends nicely with the E and A patterns we've come up with.

Try a Song

It's time to put these elements to work in a song. **"Handsome Molly"** is a traditional song that's been covered by artists from David Bromberg to Mick Jagger. It has a straightforward progression using E, A, and B chords. You can simply strum through the piece using the basic chord shapes we figured out,

or—if you want a little more of a challenge—substitute the strumming patterns in Examples 6, 7, and 8, as shown in the tab. If you're truly ambitious, you can use the fingerpicking patterns in Examples 8 and 9 in lieu of strumming.

The point of all this is to show you that taking the time to play around in an alternate tuning can give you ideas and sounds you may not otherwise experience. And you don't have to change a lot of strings. Look what we've done by changing just one string by a half step! I hope this encourages you to explore beyond standard tuning. Your guitar has more to offer than you can imagine.

TRACK 16 Ex. 10

B
x21003

Handsome Molly

Traditional, arranged by David Hodge

TRACK 17   **Played up to Speed, then Played Slowly**

Tuning: E A D F♯ B E

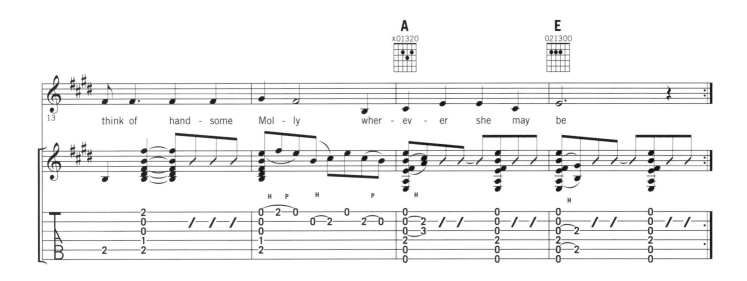

1. | **E**   **B**
   I wish I was in London or in some other seaport town

                                  A   **E**
   I'd set my foot on a steamship and sail the ocean round

                                      B
   Just sailing on the ocean, just sailing on the sea

                             A   **E**
   I'd think of handsome Molly wherever she may be

2. | **E**   **B**
   Hair as black as a raven's, eyes as black as coal

                                A   **E**
   They shine just like the lillies out in the morning's glow

                                                  B
   She goes to church on Sunday, she passed me right on by

                             A   **E**
   I could tell what she was thinking by the roving of her eye

3. | **E**   **B**
   Remember handsome Molly, you promised me your hand

                            A   **E**
   Said if you were to marry that I would be your man

                                                  B
   But now you've broken your promise, go and marry whom you please

                             A   **E**
   While my poor heart is breaking, you're lying at your ease

Repeat Verse 1

ACCOMPANIMENT IN OPEN G AND OPEN D

Mark Hanson

Singer-songwriters work hard to develop a distinctive style through their lyrics, melodic flow, and vocal delivery. But developing a distinctive guitar accompaniment style is also important. There are several ways to do this, of course, but a surprisingly easy approach is to use alternate tunings. Tunings represent a rich, nearly limitless accompaniment tool that can be wielded in ear-turning ways with relative ease.

Alternate tunings range from those in which the open strings produce a simple major chord, like open G (D G D G B D, as used by James Taylor for "Love Has Brought Me Around") and open D (D A D F# A D, as used by Joni Mitchell on "Chelsea Morning"), to tunings that seem bizarre, such as the A C C G G# C tuning used by Sonic Youth for "Candle." All of them can produce interesting and unusual harmonies and voicings created by simple fingerings, making them perfect for accompanists.

The goal of this lesson is to introduce you to a few popular alternate tunings, explain the beauty and ease of use they offer, and provide concrete examples of how to use them to accompany your songs. We will focus on open G and open D tunings and a few variants.

Open-G Tuning

Open-G tuning, which is sometimes called taropatch, Spanish, or Sebastopol tuning, is very popular among blues and slide players as well as Hawaiian slack-key guitarists and contemporary folk artists. Notable songs in open G include Nanci Griffith's "Love at the Five and Dime," Robert Johnson's "Cross Road Blues," and Eric Clapton's "Running on Faith." To get into open G from standard tuning, tune your first, fifth, and sixth strings down a whole step.

Let's get started by playing two common G chords in open-G tuning (**Example 1**). Note that the root note G is the fifth string. Harmonics sound stunning in open major (**Example 2**) and minor tunings. **Example 3** is a Gadd9 chord, a good example of how rich a chord can sound with a simple fingering. **Example 4** shows a C chord in several positions.

A great way to memorize new information quickly is to associate it with something you know. It may seem odd, but you can use some of the chord shapes you know in standard tuning to play chords in alternate tunings. In open-G tuning, the following standard-tuning chord shapes work great in many places on the neck: Am, D7, D, A7, and partial- and full-barre chords.

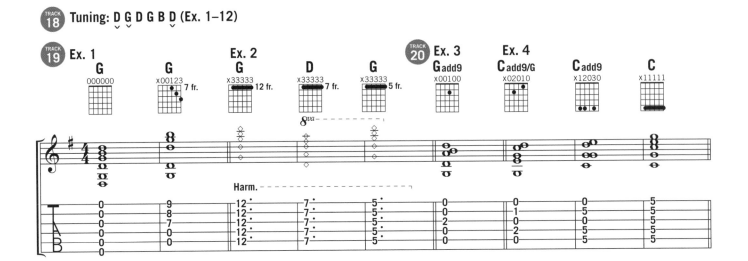

Example 5 uses the Am fingering in six places on the neck. Notice that some chords are major and some are minor. It's not all that important to know the names of all these chords when you're first trying them out. Get to know the sounds and the positions first. You can memorize the names later.

Em and Am also work as "split" fingerings, where you play an open string between what are normally adjacent string fingerings. **Example 6** uses the "split" Am fingering—fret the fifth and fourth strings with your middle and ring fingers, instead of the fourth and third strings (keep your index finger on the second string). Joni Mitchell used this shape in her song "Morning Morgantown." **Example 7** is a strumming pattern using both normal Am and split Am fingerings. You can use the Am fingerings to play in G minor (**Example 8**), even though this is G-*major* tuning.

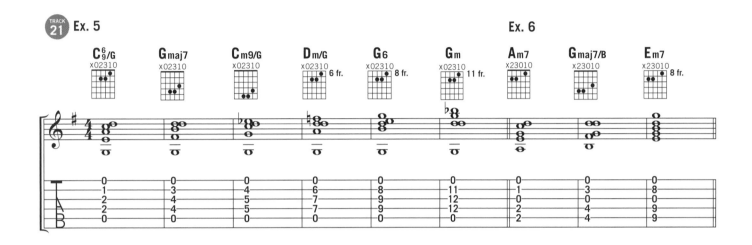

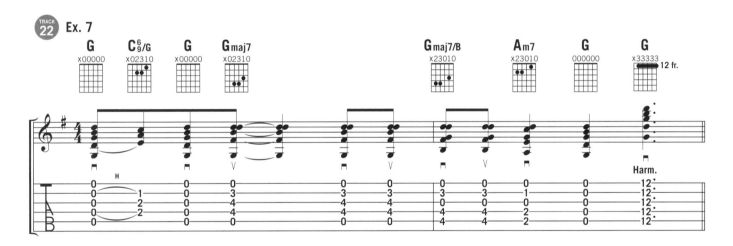

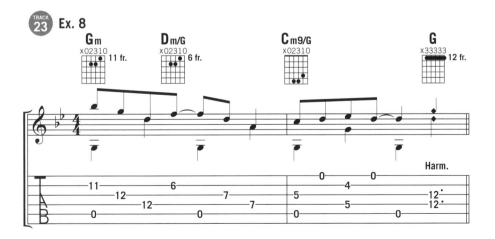

Examples **9a** and **9b** show where to use D7 and half-barre shapes. **Example 10** is a strumming pattern that uses both the D7 and half-barre shapes and sounds a bit like Chicago's "Beginnings," from the band's first recording, *Chicago Transit Authority*.

TRACK 24 **Ex. 9a: D7 Shapes**

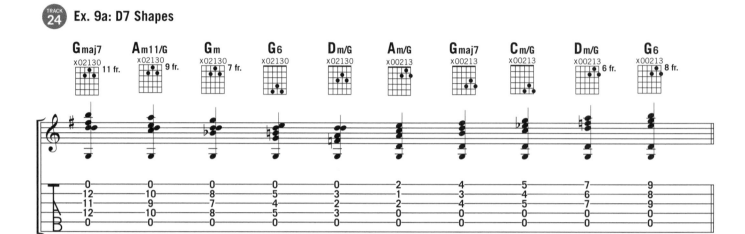

Ex. 9b: Half-Barre Shapes

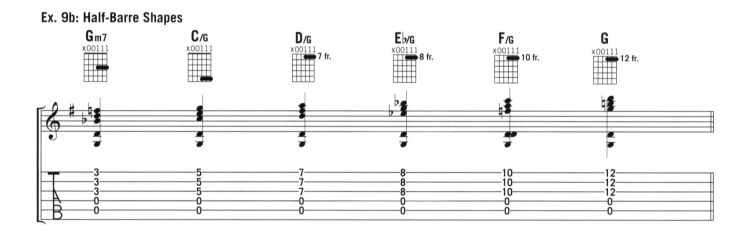

TRACK 25 **Ex. 10**

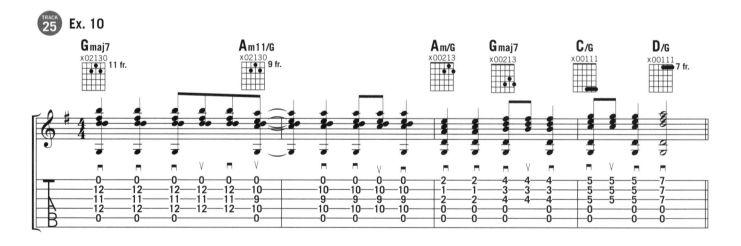

EXPLORE ALTERNATE TUNINGS

An accompanist might support a vocal melody with a flowing countermelody in the guitar, as shown in **Example 11**—an open-G fingerpicking pattern that incorporates a melodic line into the accompaniment. Measures 1–2 are played over a G chord, while measures 3–4 show positions that work well over a D chord. Try to sustain the fretted notes as long as possible. **Example 12** shows how easy it is to play the classic I–vi–ii–V chord progression in open G (think "Blue Moon" or the Beatles' "This Boy").

Open-D Tuning

Open-D tuning (D A D F♯ A D) is also very popular among singers, slide players, and instrumentalists. Well-known examples include Joni Mitchell's "Big Yellow Taxi," Richie Havens' "Handsome Johnny," and Ry Cooder's "Vigilante Man." The open strings of this tuning explicitly state a major key (D major), but with a little effort you can use open D to play in other keys. Slide and blues players often shift this tuning up a whole step to sound in E (E B E G♯ B E), which

TRACK 26 **Ex. 11**

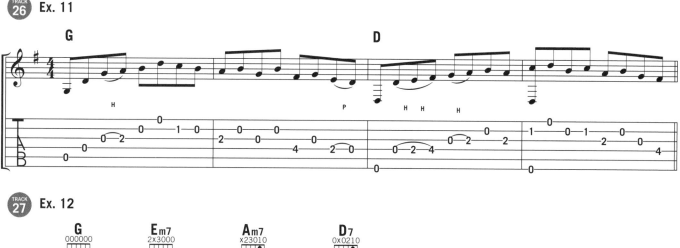

TRACK 27 **Ex. 12**

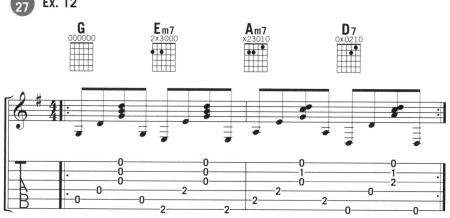

Tuning Families

Guitar tunings are usually divided into groups by letter names that suggest the keys most often associated with that tuning. D, G, and C tunings are the most common. Open E and A tunings are identical to open D and open G, respectively, except that all the strings are tuned two frets (one whole-step) higher. These higher-pitched tunings work great for slide work—they can really scream with the higher tension. Within these groups, there is a huge variety of tunings—as many as players can dream up.

D tunings like dropped D (D A D G B E), open D (D A D F♯ A D), and D A D G A D usu-ally have the root note (D) on the sixth string, an A note on the fifth string, and another D as the open fourth string. This is called "root-position" voicing, meaning that the root note is the lowest note in the bass. This root/fifth/root combination in the bass is a very powerful indicator that D is home base. Good players can use root-position voicing to play in keys other than D, however.

G tunings like open G (D G D G B D) and G6 (D G D G B E) most often have the root note on the fifth string. The lowest bass string is D—the fifth of a G chord. This is called a *chord inversion*, meaning that a note other than the root note is on the bot-tom. This is not as powerful and defining a sound as a root-position voicing, but open G is still one of the most popular tunings. To put the root note in the bass, Joni Mitchell tuned the sixth string all the way down to low G (G G D G B D) for "This Flight Tonight" from *Blue*. (Capo at the first fret if you want to play along with the recording.) Chet Atkins used G6 tuning for his version of "Vincent."

C tunings are like D in that the root is most often the lowest string in the bass. Well-known C-tuning compositions include Leo Kottke's "Busted Bicycle" (C G C G C E) and Joni Mitchell's "Coyote" (C G C E C E).

increases the tension on the strings and produces a brighter tone.

To get into D tuning, you must lower four strings from standard. Tune your sixth, second, and first strings down a whole step and your third string down a half step. If you're in open G, tune your second string down a whole step, your third string down a half step, and your fifth string back up a whole step to A.

Open D and open G actually have the same string relationships. That is, they use the same chord shapes and scale fingerings, *but moved over one string*. All the open-G fingerings you have learned so far will work in open-D tuning if you move them one string toward the bass string. For example, take the split Am fingering from Example 6 and place it on the third, fifth, and sixth strings in open-D tuning. Voilà! A lovely Em11 chord in open-D tuning.

Example 13 shows a version of each chord in the key of D. Experiment with these, playing them in different sequences, such as I–IV–V–I, I–ii–V–I, or iii–IV–ii–V, and make up progressions of your own.

Now let's apply some standard-tuning chord shapes to open D. **Example 14** shows how using E and A chord shapes on the third, fourth, and fifth strings can create a beautifully harmonized chord progression all the way up the neck. For a lovely

effect, allow the first, second, and sixth strings to drone as you change chords. To get the vii chord at the tenth and 11th frets, use a D shape. **Example 15** shows an even easier fingering, this time alternating E7 and A7 chord shapes as you go up the neck.

Example 16 shows where to find double-stop (two-note) octaves, thirds, and sixths in open D. Try strumming all six strings while you experiment with these fingerings. Partial-

barre chords also work great in open D. **Example 17** is a fingerpicking pattern that could work as a countermelody under a vocal melody. It uses a one-finger Dadd9 chord and a rich A11 sound produced by a simple Am shape. **Example 18** is a strumming pattern using two- and three-finger shapes. Strum continuous down-up eighth notes throughout, playing all six strings. There are workable triads on the treble strings, as in

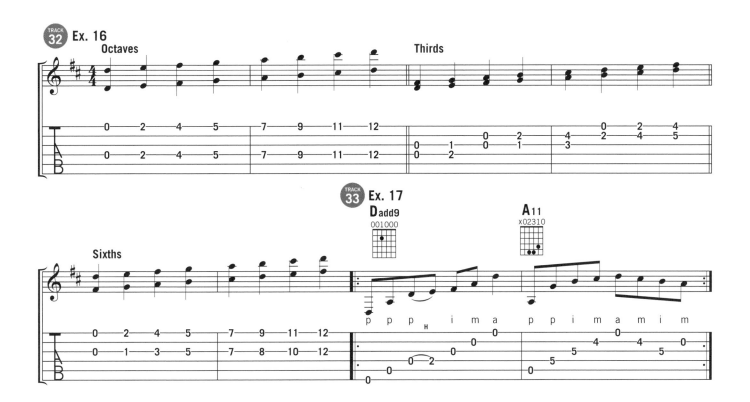

Open-C Tunings

In addition to open G and open G, you can tune to open C—where the open strings are tuned to a C chord. One version of open C is simply open D tuned down a whole step: C G C E G C. This is great if you have a low-pitched voice, or want a fat, rumbling sound from the guitar. Consider putting on strings that are of a bit heavier gauge than normal if you tune this low. There are hundreds of open-C, open-D, and open-E recordings. To get an idea of how successful singer-songwriters have used them, listen to Bruce Cockburn's "Sunwheel Dance," John Lee Hooker's version of "Terraplane Blues," Dougie

MacLean's "Caledonia," Nirvana's "Lithium," Pearl Jam's "Oceans," Chris Smither's "Mail Order Mystics," Willis Alan Ramsey's "Watermelon Man," and George Thorogood's "Woman with the Blues."

In one open-C variation, C G C G C E, the third string (G) and the high E string are left at standard pitch and the second string is raised to C. Some C tunings raise the fourth string to an E, so there are two thirds: the fourth and first strings. Slack-key patriarch Gabby Pahinui used this tuning with the second string tuned down to an A, creating a C Mauna Loa tuning (C G E G A E) for "No Ke Ano Ahiahi," from An Island Heritage.

A favorite open-C tuning of mine, C G D G B E, is called C wahine in Hawaii, meaning it includes the major seventh (B) of the C chord. Notice that C wahine maintains the four treble strings in standard tuning, while the two bass strings go down to C and G. For someone who plays a lot of chords this is fantastic. All the notes on the treble strings are in the same place as standard tuning, with the addition of two low-pitched, great sounding bass notes. Richard Thompson uses this for his tune "1952 Vincent Black Lightning," played in the key of G.

Example 19. Try droning the open sixth string under these chords. Then drone the open fifth string.

Example 20 is I–vi–ii–V again (the "Blue Moon" chord progression). But this time the chords are not strictly major or minor. They take advantage of "color" notes added to the chords. This example also has an interesting, easy-to-play bass line, courtesy of the open strings and the second fret.

Variants of Open G and Open D

By changing just one or two strings of these tunings, you can create some interesting variations. In open G, if you raise the second string (B, the third of the scale) to C (the fourth note of the scale) you get Gsus4 tuning, a higher-pitched equivalent

of D A D G A D. Martin Simpson uses Gsus4 for the traditional song "Betsy the Serving Maid." Lowering the second string to B♭ produces G-minor tuning, which John Renbourn uses for the beautiful "Mist Covered Mountains of Home." Lowering the second string to the second note of the scale, A, produces an added second or ninth (the second note of the scale in a higher octave). Nanci Griffith uses this tuning (D G D G A D) for "One of These Days" from *The Last of the True Believers*. In each of these variants, try all of the chords from the open-G examples and experiment with altering the second-string note a fret one direction or the other.

You can move strings other than the third up or down as well. Hawaiian guitarists are fond of the sweet chords pro-

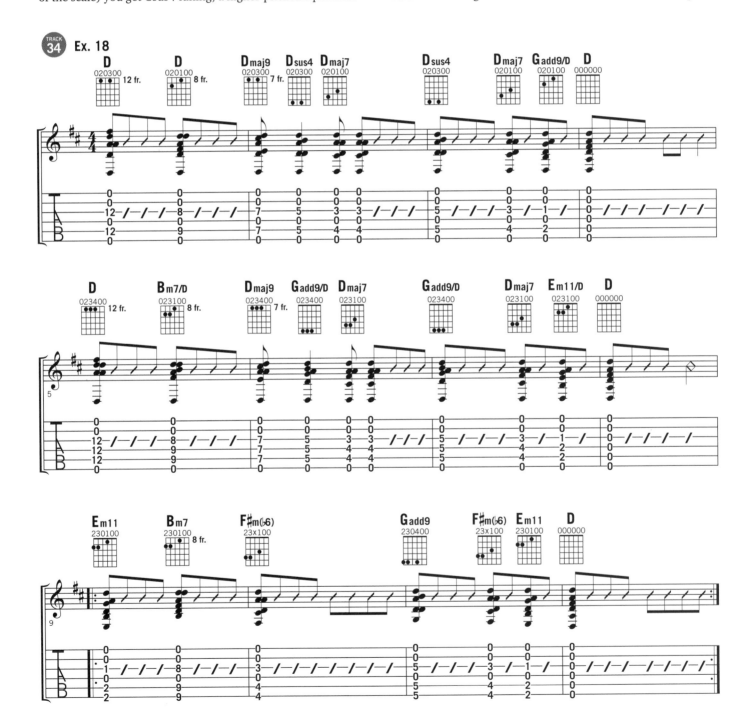

duced by adding the sixth note of the scale to a major chord; they call these sixth tunings Mauna Loa. Think of the final chord in the Beatles' "She Loves You" ("Yeah, yeah, yeah, *yeah* . . . ") and you'll recognize the sound. Hawaiian Cyril Pahinui used an open-D6 tuning (D A D F♯ B E) to record "Sanoe." To get into this tuning, raise the second string from open D back up to B, and experiment with the chord fingerings for open D. In other bluesy variations, the fifth is raised to a flatted seventh—D A D F♯ C D—or a root note is lowered to the seventh: D A D F♯ A C, which Richie Havens used for his version of Fred Neil's "The Dolphins."

By raising the major third (F♯) in open D, you get D A D G A D (see the "Intro to D A D G A D" lesson). Lowering the F♯ to the minor third (F♮) produces D-minor tuning (D A D F A D), which bluesman Skip James used for an early recording of "Hard Time Killin' Floor Blues." The third can also be lowered to the second, an E note, producing D A D E A D tuning, which Joni Mitchell used for "I Had a King," or all the way down to the root note (D), so that it is in unison with the fourth string: D A D D A D. This drone tuning

has only roots and fifths and is one of David Crosby's favorites ("Music Is Love").

Choose Your Tuning

Each tuning has a distinctive sound and creates an effect or mood—something an accompanist must consider when deciding on a tuning for a song. Think about what kind of effect you want your song to have, then choose a tuning that will enhance that feeling.

Of course, there are many more chord shapes in these tunings than the ones I've shown here. You can find more in alternate-tuning books, including Stringletter's *Alternate Tunings Guitar Essentials* as well as my own: *Complete Book of Alternate Tunings* and *Alternate Tunings Picture Chords* (accentonmusic .com). You can find online alternate-tuning calculators as well.

Hopefully you have gained some insight and inspiration from the material provided here. Don't be afraid to experiment. Put familiar shapes all over the neck. Strum lots of open strings with minimally fretted chords. And have fun!

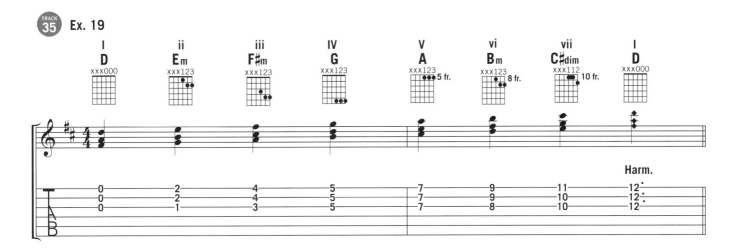

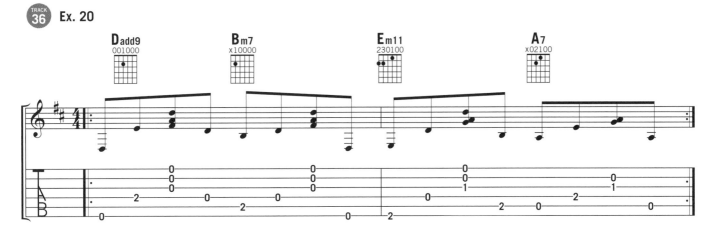

INTRO TO D A D G A D

Doug Young

Are you feeling like you're in a rut, playing the same things all the time? One of the best ways to break out of your old habits is to learn a new tuning. Alternate tunings can stimulate your creativity and provide some fresh tools for creating music, taking you in directions you may not have considered. D A D G A D, named after the open-string pitches used in the tuning, is relatively easy to learn and also has enough depth and flexibility to challenge you if you want to learn more. In this lesson, we'll explore a few common chords and scale patterns in D A D G A D—enough to get you started on both accompaniment and solo guitar.

To get your guitar tuned to D A D G A D from standard tuning, tune the sixth string down a whole step, until it sounds an octave below the fourth string. Now drop the first string until it is two octaves above the sixth string (or one octave above the fourth string). Finally, lower the second string until it sounds an octave above the fifth string. Strum the open strings, and you'll hear something like a Dsus4 chord (with an omitted third). Cool, right?

Easy I, IV, and V
A good way to get started in any alternate tuning is to find the I, IV, and V (or V7) chords of a key. In D A D G A D, you can play the I, IV, and V7 chords in the key of D—D, G, and A7—with one finger. **Example 1** shows the fingerings and a simple picking pattern. These chords may sound a little different to your ears. Part of the magic of D A D G A D is the way the open strings tend to create chord extensions that change the chord voicings a bit (see "One-Finger Chords").

One-Finger Chords
These one-finger D and A7 chords are actually missing a note—the third of the chord—giving them a sort of modal sound. The G has an A—the ninth—in it, and also has a D in the bass, making it a Gadd9/D. But you don't have to worry about these details to use the chords. To get used to the sound, try these chords—either strumming or fingerpicking—in a song you already know.

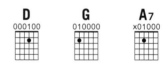

TRACK 37 Tuning: D A D G A D

TRACK 38 Ex. 1

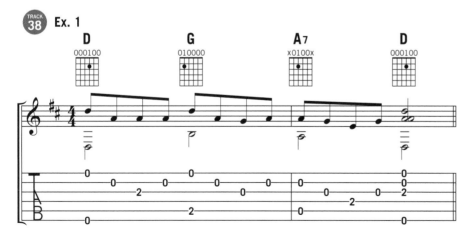

Example 2 introduces two additional fingerings for each of these chords, so you now know three chord shapes for each of the three primary chords in the key of D, each with a slightly different sound. The new D and A chords include major thirds—an F♯ in the D chord and a C♯ in the A chord—making them sound more like the chords you know from standard tuning. One of the G shapes eliminates the ninth, while the other places a low G in the bass. These shapes just give you a few more sounds to work with.

Simplify the Scales

Knowing a few scale patterns can help when you want to play melodies. **Example 3** is an extremely easy, one-octave D-major scale that only uses notes on the second and fourth frets. No complicated patterns to learn here!

Hidden within this simple scale is one of the keys to the D A D G A D sound. Look at the three notes in **Example 4**: there are three consecutive scale notes on three adjacent strings. Let these strings ring out, and listen to the sound.

TRACK **39** Ex. 2

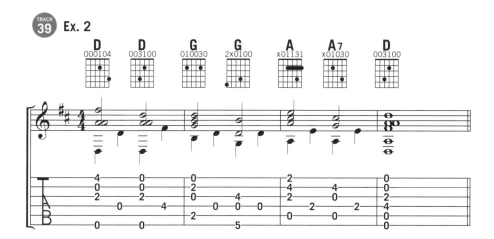

TRACK **40** Ex. 3   Ex. 4

Part of the magic of this tuning is the way the open strings tend to create chord extensions that change the chord voicings a bit.

Now revisit Example 3 and let the notes ring out the same way as much as you can.

Example 5 uses this scale to play a melody over open bass notes on the lower strings. You might want to damp the bass strings a bit, to allow the melody notes to stand out. This technique is great for fiddle tunes, Celtic melodies, and more.

This D-major scale works really well with the chord shapes we've learned. When you play **Example 6**, you'll hear a very typical D A D G A D fingerstyle sound, created by combining elements of the scale pattern in Example 3 and the basic I, IV, and V chord shapes with some hammer-ons and pull-offs to open strings. You may have noticed that none of these examples requires more than two fingers on your fretting hand. D A D G A D lets you create a lot of sound using fairly simple fingerings.

Fly Solo

With these tools in place, we can try a solo fingerstyle piece in D A D G A D. The arrangement of the Irish tune **"Down by the Salley Gardens"** on page 30 was built from the scales and

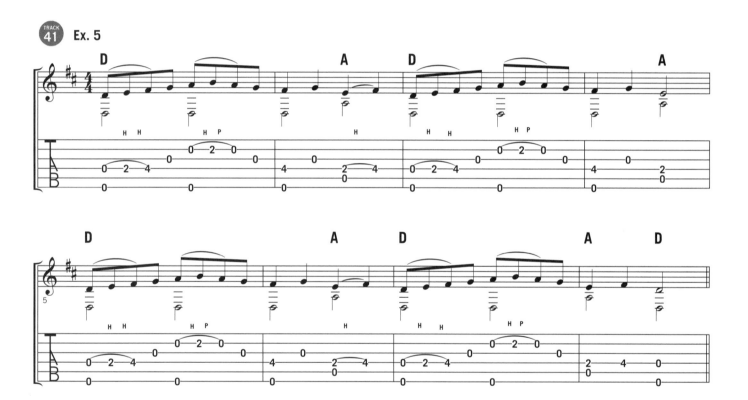

28

chords we've already discussed. The melody falls entirely within the scale pattern from Example 3, adding both bass notes and chord shapes as accompaniment. You may want to work out the chord progression before trying to play the tune. In most cases, the melody notes fall right out of the chord shapes.

The first 16 bars—one verse—are very straightforward. You should be able to find the chord shapes and scale patterns from this lesson without much trouble. The second verse introduces some variations, including grace notes (hammer-ons and pull-offs). If you find these difficult, leave them out while you learn the basic tune. You can always add them later, or try some of your own ideas.

If you stick to the scale notes and chord shapes we've used in this lesson, almost anything you play will sound good.

Notice that this arrangement takes advantage of the three-note pattern we discussed in Example 4 in several places: measures 24, 26, 28, and 32.

Explore on Your Own

Although many people think of D A D G A D as a Celtic tuning, it's more versatile than you might imagine. If you like the sound, you may want to explore the wide range of music others have created in D A D G A D. Check out the music of Pierre Bensusan, Laurence Juber, Al Petteway—even Led Zeppelin!—and many others who use D A D G A D frequently. And of course, there are many other alternate tunings waiting to be discovered as well. So dive in, explore, and have fun!

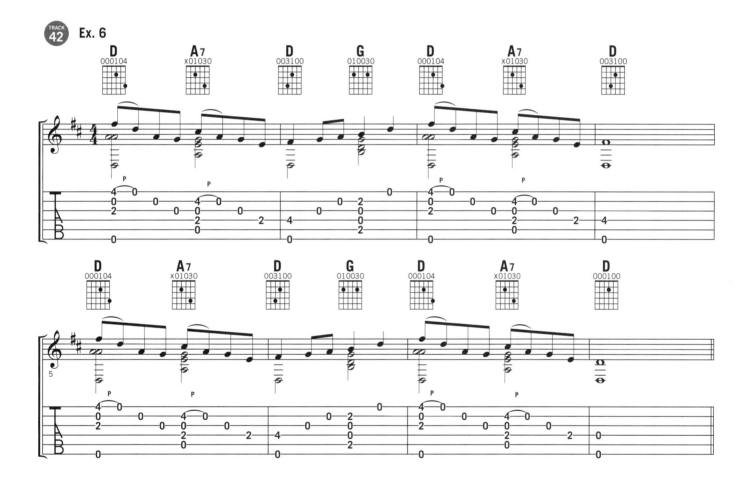

Down by the Salley Gardens

Traditional, arranged by Doug Young

 **Played up to Speed**

Tuning: D A D G A D

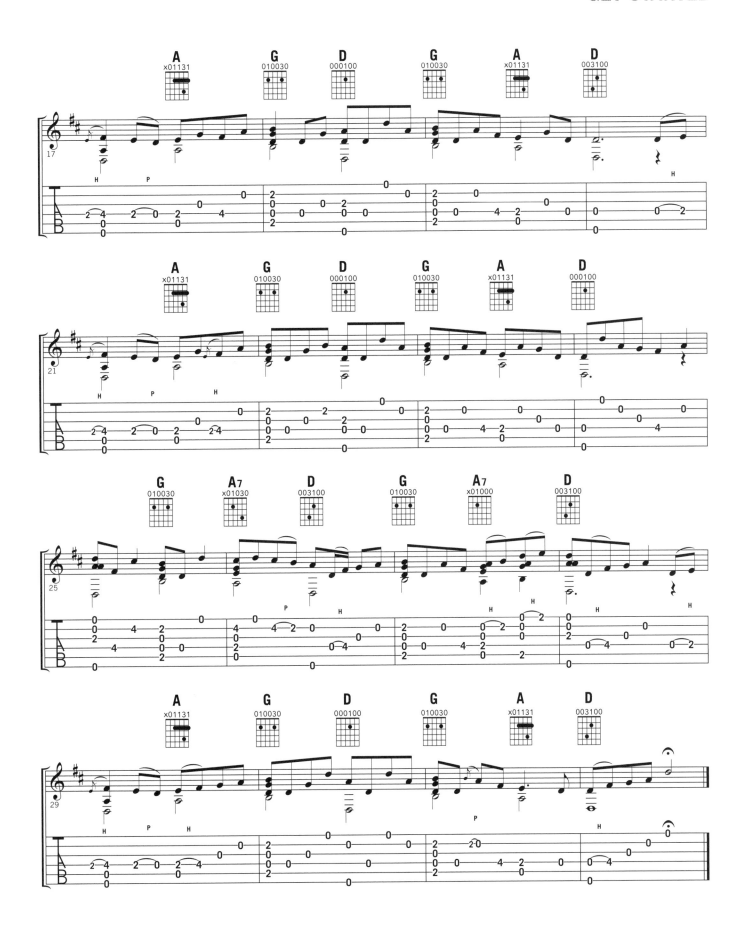

EXPLORE D A D G A D

Doug Young

In the "Intro to D A D G A D" lesson we covered the basics of D A D G A D tuning, from chords to scales. Now let's take the next step and check out two other ways to exploit the unique qualities of this tuning: creating harp-style effects and playing octaves.

Harp-Style Guitar

One technique that should be in every guitarist's bag of tricks is a method of playing that is often described as harp style, in which you maximize the number of consecutive notes being played on different strings. As a result, successive melody notes in a harp-style guitar arrangement ring out and cascade into each other. Just as with a harp, or a piano with the sustain pedal held down, the effect can create a beautiful collage of sound. Besides sounding great, the technique makes it easier to play fast passages smoothly, which is useful for playing fiddle tunes and other up-tempo pieces.

You can achieve the harp effect whether playing fingerstyle or flatpicking, and in any tuning—including standard—but it works especially well in D A D G A D. One of the reasons that harp style works so well in D A D G A D is that the open

> With harp-style technique, you maximize the number of consecutive notes being played on different strings.

second and third strings are adjacent scale tones, which makes it easier to find fingerings that sustain sequential notes. For example, you can sustain three sequential notes of a scale by fingering an F♯ on the fourth string while playing the open G and A (third and second) strings (**Example 1**). By themselves, minor- and major-second intervals tend to sound like an ugly clash, but when playing melodically, this same dissonance creates a beautiful harp-like sound that you don't get when playing the same notes sequentially on the same string.

Example 2 shows a simple way to play a D-major scale in D A D G A D. You can create the harp effect here by continuing to hold the notes on the fourth fret of the second and fourth strings after plucking them. Notice that the middle

TRACK 44 Tuning: **D A D G A D**

TRACK 45 Ex. 1   Ex. 2

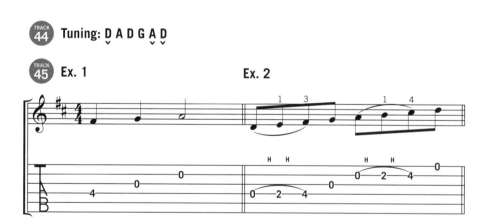

three notes of this scale are the same as the notes in Example 1. Now, let's rearrange this scale to prevent any consecutive notes from being played on the same string. Move the E to the fifth string and the B to the third string, as in **Example 3**, and you have a very playable, harp-style D-major scale.

Pay close attention to the fingerings and try to play the line as smoothly as possible, making sure that every note rings as long as possible and that you don't lift any fingers until you absolutely need to. If you plant your fingers before you play the note they're fretting, you will get an even smoother sound. Notice in Example 3 that the E and B notes sound higher than the notes that precede them (D and A, respectively) but are played on lower strings! This is common in harp-style playing and becomes second nature with practice.

It is useful to have multiple ways to finger these patterns, both to facilitate different melodies and to create slightly different effects, depending on which notes are sustained against each other. **Example 4** shows yet another way to play the D-major scale in Examples 2 and 3 and offers an opportunity to practice shifting positions smoothly while sustaining notes as

long as possible. Try to hold the fourth-fret F♯ with your index finger as you stretch your pinky up to the B on the ninth fret.

There are many cases where you cannot play every successive scale note on an adjacent string, but hammer-ons and pull-offs can be an effective alternative if played smoothly while you keep other notes ringing. **Example 5** demonstrates this by extending the D-major scale in Example 4.

Although it's important to pay attention to fretting-hand fingerings, don't completely ignore your picking hand. Whether you're fingerpicking or flatpicking, focus on creating a smooth sound and avoid cutting off any notes prematurely. Some of the patterns will also require some time to get used to, due to higher notes played on lower strings and unexpected jumps between strings.

Harp-Style Patterns in Other Keys

Harp-style scale patterns in D A D G A D can also be found in keys other than D. **Example 6** is a partial G-major scale pattern, which can be played over a G bass if you are playing fingerstyle. This pattern begins on the fifth of the key (D),

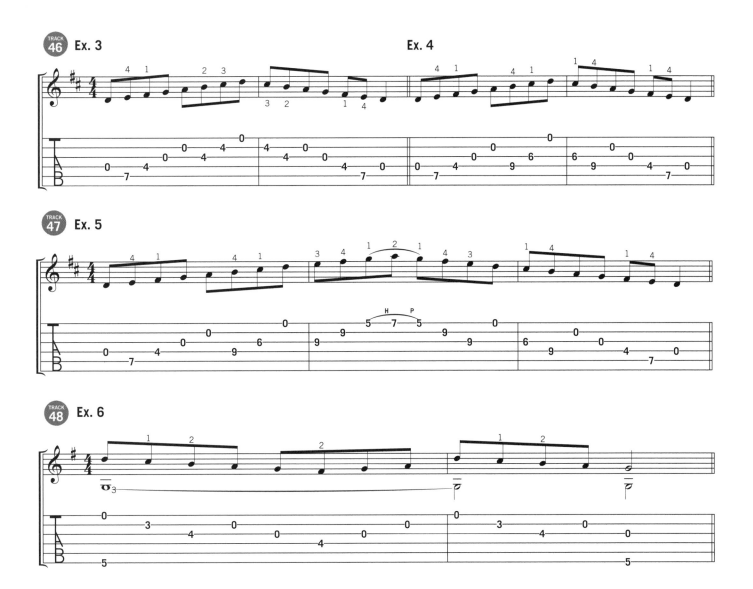

moving down as far as the seventh (F♯) before ending on the root. Here we're taking advantage of D A D G A D's close second and third strings to easily sustain two scale tones that are a minor-second apart. The descending A-major scale in **Example 7** begins with a pull-off. If the stretch in this example is too difficult, try the alternate fingering in **Example 8**. Make sure to sustain the second note (G♯) while playing the second pull-off to continue the harp effect. **Example 9** is similar to Example 4 but is in D minor.

There are an infinite number of scales and patterns waiting to be explored, in many different keys. Having these scale patterns under your fingers in various keys is good preparation for playing melodies. The harp sound is most effective during scalar passages, and the cross-string technique also makes the fast scale-like patterns often found in fiddle tunes easier to play.

Playing Melodies

Now let's apply the harp technique to a melody. Unlike using simple scales, creating a harp-like arrangement is a bit like putting a puzzle together, and figuring out where to place each note may require some compromises. **"Whiskey Before Breakfast"** is a well-known old-time fiddle tune that also shows up at Celtic *seisiúns*. You can play this tune fingerstyle or with a pick, although the second half of this arrangement adds bass notes that work best when played fingerstyle.

The first two measures use the same notes as the scale pattern in Example 3, although the hammer-on in measure 2 requires a bit of extra planning. Sustain the F♯ on the fourth string during the hammer-on to maintain the harp-style effect. Measure 3 is a little challenging because of the position change. The smoothest approach is to maintain your hand

position from measure 2 through the first note of measure 3, so that the sustaining quarter note masks the move down to second position on the second beat of measure 3. Return to your previous position by grabbing the last note of measure 3 (F♯) with your index finger and shifting positions while the open second string is ringing. You can play the fourth note of measure 3 with your ring finger, but using your middle finger creates an even smoother transition.

The B section of "Whiskey Before Breakfast," which begins at measure 9, presents a new arranging challenge. Harp style is most effective on scale-like melodies, but the B section includes a few jumps of a fourth (measures 9 and 11). To maintain as much of the harp effect as possible in measure 9, you can play notes of the same pitch on different strings—notice that the D and A notes are played both on the open first and second strings and at the seventh fret of the third and fourth strings. Measure 11 uses a different approach, adding an open D on the first string between melody notes. This note is not part of the melody, but if played lightly, helps maintain the harp sound.

The added bass notes in the second pass through the melody (beginning in measure 17) require a few fingering adjustments. Measure 20 breaks out of the cross-string pattern and uses some slides and pull-offs to allow the open A bass note to sustain, and measure 27 requires some significant fingering adjustments because of the fretted G bass note.

"Whiskey Before Breakfast" can be played slow and pretty or fast and blazing. Once you see how the harp technique works, try it with your own favorite tunes. Harp style can be effective on anything from fiddle tunes to pop tunes, so explore and have fun!

TRACK 49 Ex. 7   **Ex. 8**

TRACK 50 Ex. 9

Whiskey Before Breakfast

Traditional, arranged by Doug Young

 Played up to Speed

Tuning: D A D G A D

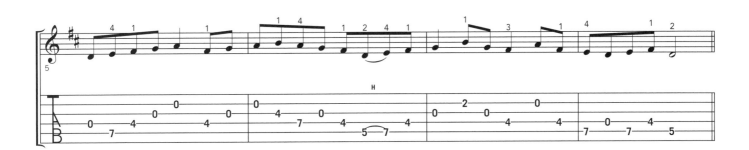

Octaves in D A D G A D

You may have heard the sound of octaves on recordings by jazz guitarists Django Reinhardt, Wes Montgomery, George Benson, Lee Ritenour, and others. Octaves are a great way to beef up a bass line or add a distinctive texture to a melody. D A D G A D tuning not only offers many opportunities to use octaves but also allows you to play some things you simply could not play in standard tuning.

One reason octaves are so useful in D A D G A D is that octaves are easily accessible on three pairs of strings. In this tuning, the sixth and fourth strings and fourth and first strings (all D notes) are an octave apart, and the fifth and second strings, both tuned to A, are also an octave apart. So no matter where you are on the fretboard, you can easily play an octave above or below any string except the G string by simply adding a note on the same fret, two or three strings over.

Example 10 shows a single-note scale fragment in D A D G A D on the sixth string. **Example 11** shows the same line in octaves; simply finger the same frets on both the sixth and fourth strings. You might try fingering the lower string with your second finger and the higher string with your third finger, although other fingerings are possible as well. **Example 12**

demonstrates octaves on the fifth and second strings, and **Example 13** shows octaves on the fourth and first strings. Notice that there is one unused string between the octaves when you play on the fourth and sixth strings but two empty strings when playing octaves on the fifth and second strings or fourth and first strings. With a little practice, you will get used to the difference. **Example 14** puts this all together with a two-octave D-major scale in octaves. You may also want to pick out scales in other keys.

If you are playing fingerstyle, you can pick the lower note of the octave with your right-hand thumb, but you may also want to practice playing both strings with your fingers, which will free your thumb to add bass notes. You can also play these examples with a pick, but you'll need to damp the strings in the middle with your fretting hand.

So far, we've seen that octaves are easy to play in D A D G A D, but we haven't yet played anything that couldn't be done in standard tuning. Because octaves are on parallel frets in D A D G A D, it's easy to play hammer-ons and pull-offs in octaves using the open strings. This would be hard, if not impossible, to do in standard tuning because there are no octaves on open strings in standard tuning (the high and low

E strings span two octaves). **Example 15** combines hammer-ons and pull-offs for a slightly syncopated, percussive-sounding line. To play this line, hammer onto each fretted pair of notes from the open strings, and then pull off from the fretted notes to the open strings. Pick only the first notes on each string; all other notes are played with pull-offs or hammer-ons. Notice that hammer-ons and pull-offs are easiest to do with open strings. It is possible to hammer on and pull off between fretted notes by barring the lower pair of notes with your index finger and playing a higher pair of notes with your third and fourth fingers, but the fingering is difficult and the effect is less dramatic.

You can also slide between any pair of fretted notes in octaves, as in the line in **Example 16**. Combining slides with hammer-ons and pull-offs can create some complex-sounding lines that are fairly easy and fun to play (**Example 17**). When playing this lick, your picking hand picks only three notes: the open strings that start each five-note phrase.

These examples are probably best played fingerstyle, but it's also possible to use octaves effectively when strumming. Try letting the open strings ring while creating a moving line with the fingered octaves, as in **Example 18**, which can be strummed with your hand or a flatpick. Measures 1 and 2 are basically an A chord, so avoid hitting the low D. In measure 3,

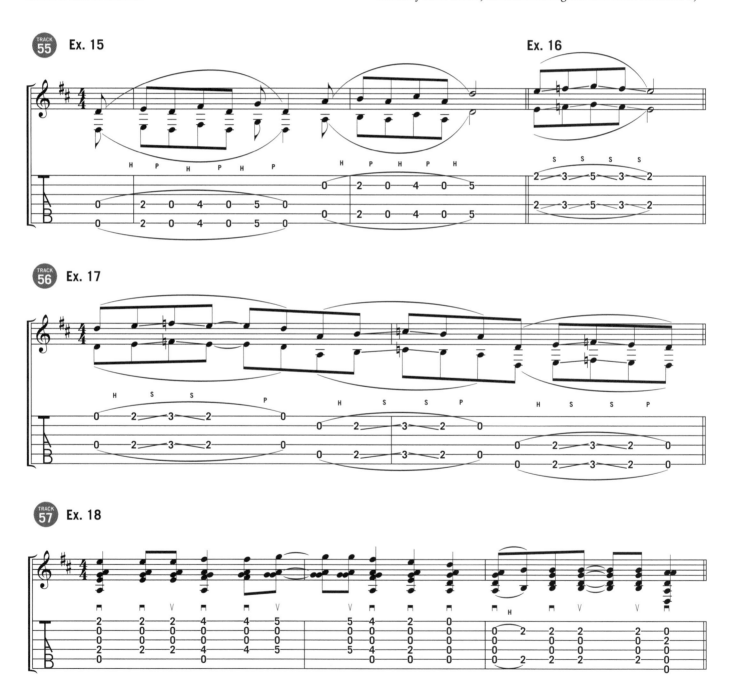

the harmony moves to a G chord with a B in the bass before resolving to a D chord on the last beat.

Using Octaves in a Song

Finally, let's take a look at how you can use these techniques in context. **"Octave Blues"** (page 40) is a 12-bar blues based almost entirely on octaves. Try to keep the bass line going with a shuffle feel, using your right-hand thumb, while playing the melody in octaves with the fingers of your right hand. Measure 5 can be a bit tricky. You can cut off the G on the fifth fret of the sixth string in time to reach the octave melody notes on beats two and three, or you may want to try playing the bass note with your pinky while playing the octaves by barring with your index finger. Using a barre allows you to hold out the bass note through the entire measure, but this can be a bit of a stretch for some hands. Measure 11 uses octaves to simulate a typical blues turnaround, ending with an octave bass run in measure 12 that leads back into the next chorus.

The second chorus (beginning at measure 13) expands on the first chorus, primarily by adding extra notes between the octaves. Jazz guitarist George Benson often added fourths and fifths in the middle of his octaves, creating a fatter, more distinctive sound, and we can emulate that sound in D A D G A D. The simplest way to add notes is to combine an open string with the fingered octave notes. Example 9 showed

one way of using open strings with octaves, but this time we'll be more selective. Some open strings may not sound right with every pair of octaves, so you'll have to use your ear and experiment to find notes that sound right to you. The first few measures of the second chorus demonstrate several situations where the open second string works well with the octaves.

You can also add fretted notes to the octaves. The easiest way to do this is to add notes between the octaves on the same fret. In the first half of measures 18 and 22, instead of just playing the octaves on the fourth and first strings, barre and play all the notes on the fourth through first strings. This creates a distinctive-sounding parallel harmony that breaks up the monotony of the octaves in the rest of the example. If you play the bass notes with your pinky, you can play the melody line smoothly by barring with your index finger.

Measure 21 shows one way to use octaves as a departure point for more complex lines, while measure 23 uses a similar idea to create a bluesy-sounding turnaround. Measure 22 is a bit challenging. To play this measure as it is intended, slide the entire barre from the third fret to the second fret, and then pull off from the barre to sound all four open strings. Finally, measure 24 adds notes between the octaves on the bass strings. Adding the note on the fifth string between an octave on the sixth and fourth string produces what rock players call a power chord, a strong ending to this piece.

Octave Blues

Music by Doug Young

58 "Octave Blues" Intro

59 Played up to Speed, Then Played Slowly

Tuning: D A D G A D

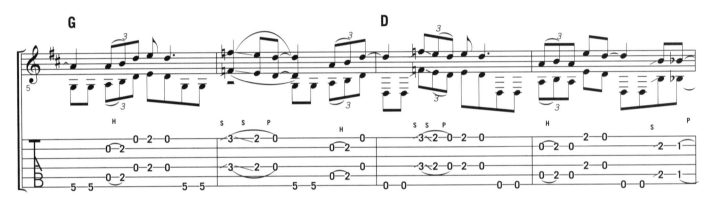

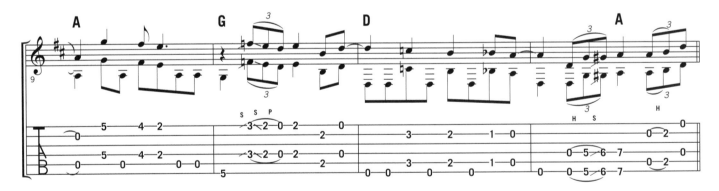

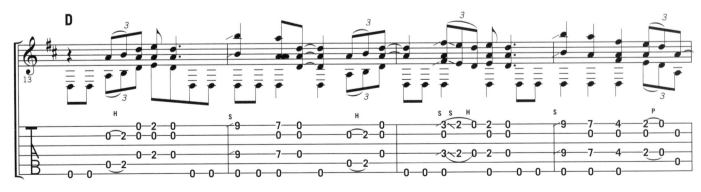

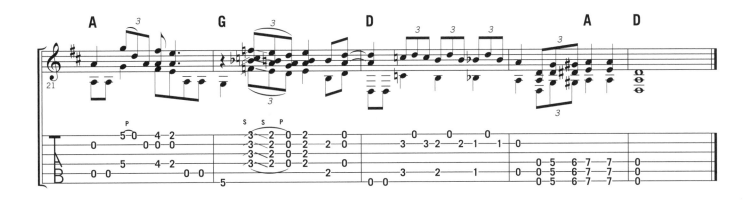

HAWAIIAN SLACK-KEY GUITAR

Fran Guidry

Slack-key guitar has its origins in Hawaii during the 1800s, when Hawaiian cowboys developed a style that provided simultaneous bass, rhythm, and lead. The English translation of a Hawaiian phrase, *ki ho'alu*, slack-key simply means "loosen the key." Slack-key is the product of Hawaiian composers and performers adapting instruments, styles, and musical concepts from other parts of the world—a process that has been going on since Europeans began visiting the islands.

People often describe slack-key tunes as relaxing or soothing. The Hawaiian term for this sweet, soothing quality is *nahenahe*, one of the key elements of an authentic slack-key sound. In this lesson, I will provide you with tips that will help you create that nahenahe feeling for your listeners and for yourself.

Loosen Up (Your Strings)

You can play slack-key on any kind of guitar. Great artists in the field have used steel-string flattops, archtops, nylon-string guitars, 12-string guitars, and even electric guitars. Slack-key is played fingerstyle, with different artists choosing bare fingers, thumbpicks, and/or fingerpicks.

There are many tunings used in this style, but the most widely used is open G, or *taropatch* tuning. From low to high, the strings are tuned D G D G B D. You can see that this tuning involves lowering the first, fifth, and sixth strings one whole step. Strumming the open strings results in a full, rich G major chord.

The bass string accompaniment is an important part of the slack-key sound. In taropatch tuning, the bass pattern for the G chord alternates between the fifth and fourth strings, while the pattern for the D chord uses the sixth and fourth strings. **Example 1** puts the two together. You'll have a more laid-back, nahenahe sound if you let the bass strings ring freely rather than damping as you might in blues or other Western styles.

A harmonized G major scale played along first and third strings (**Example 2**) can be used to produce many sweet licks. **Example 3** combines ideas from Examples 1 and 2, showing

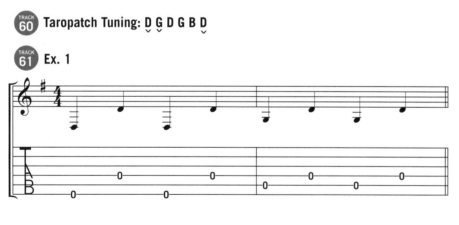

TRACK 60 Taropatch Tuning: D G D G B D

TRACK 61 Ex. 1

TRACK 62 Ex. 2   **TRACK 63** Ex. 3

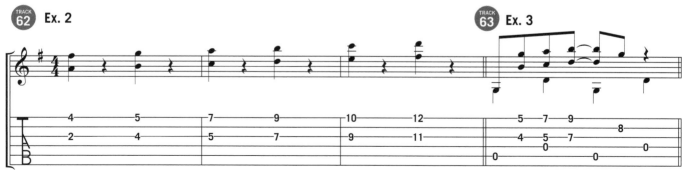

how the bass and melody can fit together as the hand moves from one G-chord position to another. The secret to a smooth island sound is to keep your fingers pressing down between notes, holding each note as long as possible before moving to the next.

The Hawaiian Turnaround

If you play with experienced Hawaiian musicians, you'll hear the term *vamp* used quite often—it's their name for the Hawaiian turnaround. The bass pattern shown in Example 1 provides the foundation—in the key of G, a vamp is one measure of D7 followed by one measure of G. Like a blues turnaround, this musical element signals the end of a verse, but unlike the blues, the Hawaiian turnaround is generally repeated a second time whenever it occurs. There are many traditional turnarounds, and different slack-key tunings are characterized by slightly different vamps. **Example 4** illustrates a descending turnaround based on the harmonized scale from Example 2. Play this figure without damping the strings for a nice, legato sound.

In taropatch tuning, another common set of turnarounds is built on a melody ascending across the strings. **Example 5** demonstrates the simplest such line. Most Hawaiian musi-

cians emphasize playing "from the heart"—adding your own personality and emotion to the music. **Example 6** shows some of the possibilities, taking the same melodic line from Example 5 a step further with an extra note and a little rhythmic displacement.

Add Expressiveness with Slurs

Many great slack-key players make liberal use of slurs—fretting-hand playing tricks common to other guitar styles—to achieve a singing, vocal quality in their playing. Look again at the fourth beat of Example 6. This upward slide from one note to another is a simple, common, and expressive slur. Downward slides are also used occasionally and can be short or long. Hammer-ons and pull-offs are also very popular among slack-key guitarists, imitating the vocal gymnastics of Hawaiian falsetto singing. **Example 7** explores a few of those ideas, including a trill on the second half of beat one, a pull-off on the end of beat two, a hammer-on on beat three, and a slide to close out the first measure. At the end of the figure, the fretting hand plays a harmonic by gently touching the strings directly above the 12th fret, another common feature in slack-key.

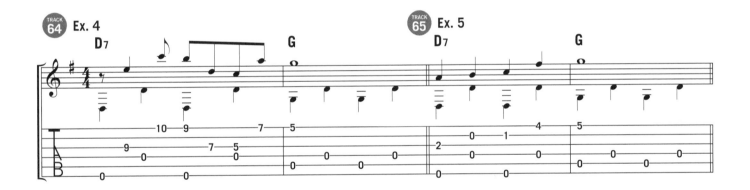

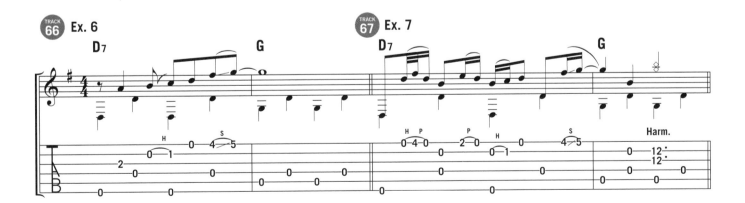

Salomila

Traditional, arranged by Fran Guidry

 TRACK 68 **Played up to Speed**

Taropatch Tuning: D G D G B D

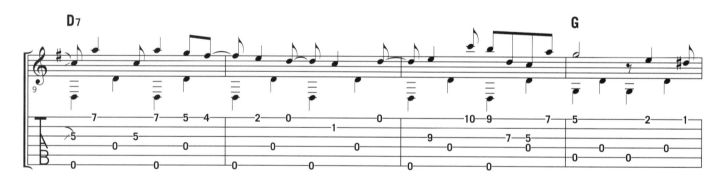

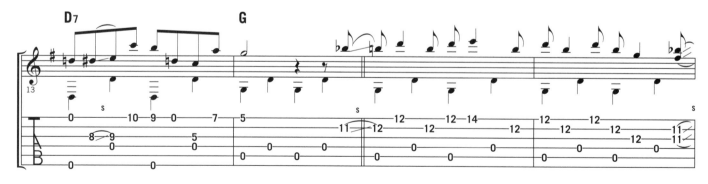

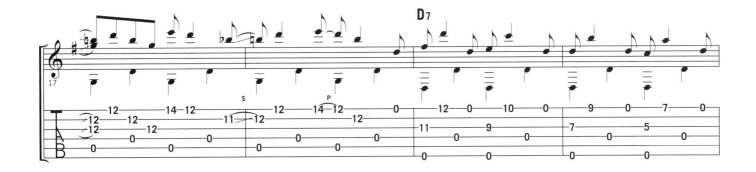

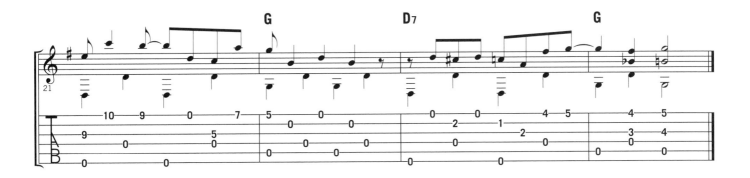

Shine Your Light on Me, Salomila

"**Salomila**" is a traditional slack-key song based on an old Tahitian melody. As in many slack-key songs, the basic harmony is simple, making use of only the G and D7 chords. The transcription takes you through two verses of the piece, showing several of the elements I've talked about.

Bars 1 through 4 are a typical slack-key intro, consisting of two consecutive turnarounds. Notice the use of the open first-string D in measure 3. Melodic use of open strings is another good way to keep your playing sounding relaxed and fluid. Ascending slides are the defining sound, along with the same harmonized scale patterns discussed previously. Bars 11 through 14 contain two more consecutive turnarounds. Starting in bar 15, the second verse is a variation of the first, this time played around the 12th fret. Use a partial barre on the first three strings, and the licks will be right under your fingers.

The descending section in bars 19 and 20 uses the D on the open first string to add interest to the harmonized scale run. The song winds up in bars 21–24 with two final turnarounds.

If you are interested in hearing more slack-key guitar, look for recordings on the Dancing Cat label, or any record-

> Loosen your strings and think about warm island weather with this soothing, laid-back style.

ings by artists such as Ledward Kaapana, Keola Beamer, Cyril Pahinui, Sonny Chillingworth, George Kuo, Ozzie Kotani, Leonard Kwan, and Gabby Pahinui.

C G D G B E TUNING

Sean McGowan

Acoustic guitarists in all genres often use alternate tunings. Some of these tunings have become so prevalent that they practically identify their genre—for example, open-D or open-G tuning for slide blues or D A D G A D for Celtic styles. This lesson will focus on the C G D G B E tuning (sometimes known as Hawaiian wahine slack-key tuning), which lends itself quite nicely to a variety of styles. We'll explore this tuning's many sonic and practical advantages, including: an expanded lower range; huge, lush, easy-to-play chord voicings; and relatively simple adaptation, since the top four strings remain the same as in standard tuning. The tuning also allows for easy soloing, because familiar scale and lead patterns are still intact (as opposed to, for example, D A D G A D, which requires a lot more practice before one is comfortable improvising in it).

Get in Tune

Let's get started by tuning down. Drop the low E and A strings down to C and G, respectively. Then double-check the top four strings, since they will likely go slightly out of tune when you lower the bottom two strings. (This is still a relatively quick tuning adjustment, one that can be easily done between songs on a gig.) Try playing octaves (**Example 1**) to check the intonation of the two bass strings. Finally, test the bottom three strings with an open triad (**Example 2**) and adjust them until it sounds good to your ear.

> C G D G B E tuning can enhance huge-sounding chords and bass lines you can't play in standard tuning.

Huge, Easy Chords

This tuning allows for some great-sounding low-register chords that resonate like a baritone guitar. Check out how full these basic chords sound:

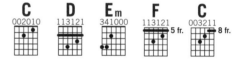

Here are a few barre-chord shapes. These chord shapes are larger in range than their standard-tuning counterparts, and most of them are easier to play:

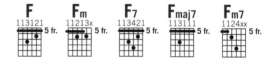

TRACK 69 Tuning: C G D G B E

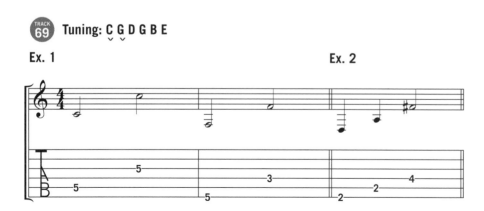

Here are some basic three-note structures with the roots on the bottom string. These are all in E♭, but the shapes are all movable:

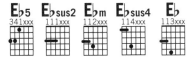

It will just take a little time to learn the notes on the two bottom strings. However, for those of you who play mandolin or bouzouki, the stacked-fifths tuning of the bottom three strings will be familiar. Notice how big the E♭-major and -minor triads sound! That's because they're open triads—the distance between notes is larger than an octave and results in a spread-out voicing. These sound like piano voicings. Listen to the sound of the common progression in **Example 3**.

Next, let's look at some four- and five-note chord voicings. (Again, all are movable forms.) They sound enormous on an acoustic, due to the two-octave range of the voicing with few, if any, repeated notes. And they're a lot easier to play than standard barre chords.

Four-Note Chords

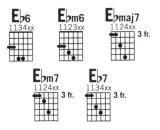

Five-Note Chords

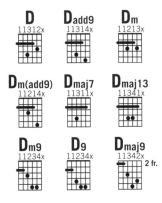

Example 4 is reminiscent of parallel dominant-ninth chords in Debussy's piano music.

So far, we've only looked at chords with sixth-string roots. Below are some shapes where the root is on the fifth string. You will recognize the upper structure of each chord on the D, G and B strings. Like chords with a root on the sixth string, these are easier to play than the standard barre forms. They even allow for voicings that are difficult to play in standard tuning.

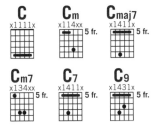

TRACK 70 Ex. 3

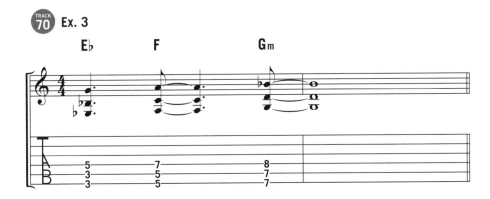

TRACK 71 Ex. 4

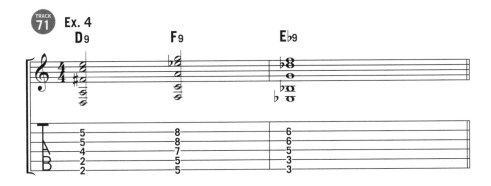

Low Bass Adds Flexibility

Some players use seven-string guitars to get low bass lines, but you can approximate this sound with the low bass tones of C G D G B E tuning. **Example 5** features a chord progression in a Brazilian samba style. The lowered bass strings give you a wider range, thereby distinguishing the bass and chord parts from one another. This flexibility allows you to sound more like two players while enabling deliciously low bass notes for fills and lines. **Example 6** illustrates this concept in a Chet Atkins style. These types of chords sound equally good with or without a bass player on the gig.

Example 7 shows a simple bass line that connects two chords in an R&B-type progression. This kind of approach is great if you're playing in a solo or duo situation.

Try a Song

"Fannie Poer" (aka "Fanny Power") is a popular piece from the 17th–18th-century Irish composer Turlough O'Carolan. The melody comes from Edward Bunting's *Ancient Music of Ireland*, and the beautiful playing of New England guitarist David Surette inspired this arrangement (page 50).

Some fingerstyle arrangements use downstemmed notes to show what's picked by your thumb and upstemmed notes to show what's picked by your fingers. In this arrangement, I wanted to highlight the melody, so I've stemmed the melody up and the accompaniment down. This means that not all downstemmed notes are played with the thumb. Observe the overall sustaining, lyrical quality—think music for Irish harp—and the quick pull-off grace notes and trills characteristic of Irish phrasing. Pay attention to the fingerings and position shifts in measures 21–23 and the natural harmonics in measure 29. Bars 10 and 11 feature five-note chords plucked with your thumb, index, middle, and ring fingers. The bottom two strings are plucked with the thumb and the ring finger plays the top string.

Fannie Poer

Music by Turlough O'Carolan, arranged by Sean McGowan

TRACK 75 **Played up to Speed**

Tuning: C G D G B E

slowly ♩ = 80–85

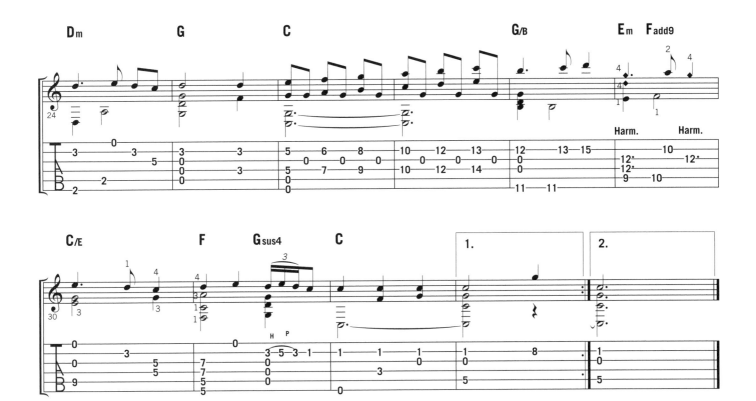

ORKNEY TUNING

Steve Baughman

For a lot of folks, retuning their strings is about as attractive as shuffling around the letters on their computer keyboard. Americans who have tried to send an e-mail from a European café know the feeling well. The question always looms: why bother with an exotic tuning when there is still so much to learn about standard E A D G B E? Give me just a few minutes here—that's all it will take to get you hooked on Orkney tuning. The tuning itself is simple: from bass to treble, the notes are C G D G C D—two C's, two G's, and two D's. Unlike D A D G A D, this tuning is impossible to pronounce, so I decided to name it after the beautiful islands off the northern coast of Scotland. This was especially fitting since I came up with the tuning while trying to arrange a Scottish song for guitar.

In this lesson I will provide you with a few simple chords and riffs that will quickly give you a sense of how Orkney can sing for you, both harmonically and melodically. I suspect you'll like what you hear yourself doing.

Orkney in the Key of G

The key of G is the most popular key people use when playing in Orkney tuning. **Example 1** shows a single-finger G chord, played without the low bass string, as well as a slightly meatier G chord that adds the fifth fret of the first string.

Example 2 shows two ways to play C, the IV chord in the key of G. The first is a simple two-finger C, followed by one of my favorite Orkney chords: a booming C5. This chord contains just C's and G's and is neither major nor minor, so it can be used in place of both C-major and -minor chords, or when neither is preferred. **Example 3** shows how easy it is to turn this chord into a major or a minor chord with a small movement of your free index finger. You can even add the major or minor sevenths without a problem, as in **Example 4**. All of these can be created with a very convenient move of the index finger—without leaving the C position in Example 2—a full five different chord possibilities out of one position.

All we need now to play simple I–IV–V patterns in the key of G is the V chord, D. The first D chord in **Example 5** sounds great on just the first four strings, although if you're comfortable fretting bass notes with your thumb, you can also try grabbing the fifth and sixth strings at the second fret for a fuller sound. The second D chord is simply the two-finger C chord from Example 2, barred at the second fret.

With just these three chords (the I, IV, and V chords in the key of G), you can play hundreds of songs in Orkney tuning. **Example 6** shows a simple exercise that includes a few of the chord shapes from this section. Try it out and then see if you can come up with a few of your own!

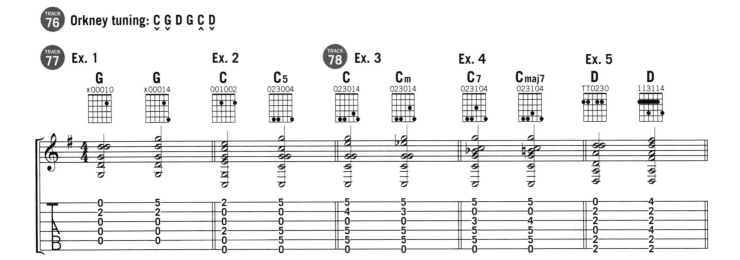

TRACK 76 Orkney tuning: C G D G C D

TRACK 77 Ex. 1   Ex. 2   TRACK 78 Ex. 3   Ex. 4   Ex. 5

Playing in C and D

While some popular tunings (like open C, open G, and open D) pretty much limit you to playing in one key, Orkney is more versatile, allowing you to play in at least three different keys with ease—all without a capo.

The key of C works very well with Orkney, and it's a convenient place to continue since we already know how to play C and G, the I and V. In fact, the two F chords in **Example 7** are enough to get us playing I–IV–V patterns in this new key. The first is a nice chord for vocal and instrument accompaniment, played on just the top four strings. If you want a thicker-sounding chord, try the barred F—the simple two-finger C chord barred at the fifth fret.

The key of D is also close by, and we already know the D and G chords (the I and IV). **Example 8** shows the A chord—the V of D. You can also create an A chord by barring the

C-major chord at the ninth fret. This gets a bit high up the neck for me, but it is worth having the option to play an A chord this way from time to time.

D A D G A D Players Rejoice!

Alternate-tuning aficionados may notice that the intervals between the first five strings in Orkney are identical to strings two through six in D A D G A D. This simple one-string shift can help make Orkney a breeze for seasoned D A D G A D veterans. For example, just as D A D G A D players can fret a D chord with just one finger (on the second fret of the third string), the one-finger G chord in Orkney is just one string higher (on the second fret of the second string). Many other D A D G A D shapes transfer just as easily—experiment for yourself!

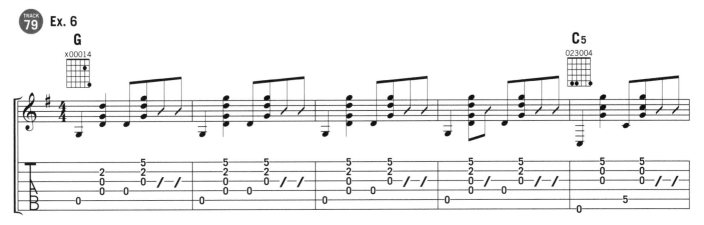

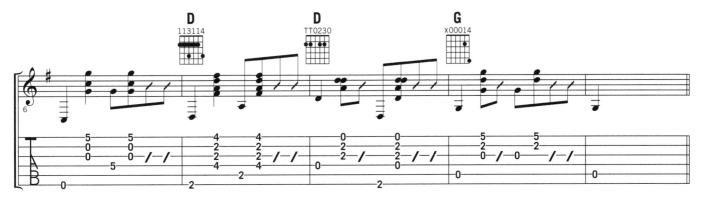

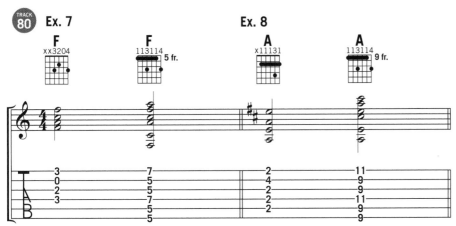

Riffs and Melodies

Now that we've learned enough chords to get started in three different keys, let's try picking out a few melodies. As you might imagine, each of these three Orkney-friendly keys has its own unique advantages when it comes to creating melody lines.

The key of G is a comfortable place to start, since the I, IV, and V chord roots (G, C, and D) are all playable on open bass strings, an added benefit not found in many other altered tunings. **Example 9a** is a short G riff I invented to get you primed for picking out melodies in Orkney. I like this

riff because it uses I, IV, and V chords and exposes you to cross-picking. If you want to make this sound a bit spooky or sad, simply flat the B note on the third string and make your first-string F♯ an F♮, as in **Example 9b**. This gives the riff a minor quality, and because your bass notes are on open strings, the fingering should be quite accessible.

Due in part to that low C on the sixth string, the key of C is also a great place to play riffs and melodies. **Example 10** will help get you started. The rich low sound of this key lends itself well to some seriously bluesy riffs, like the one shown in **Example 11**. Just like in the key of G, the key of C makes it

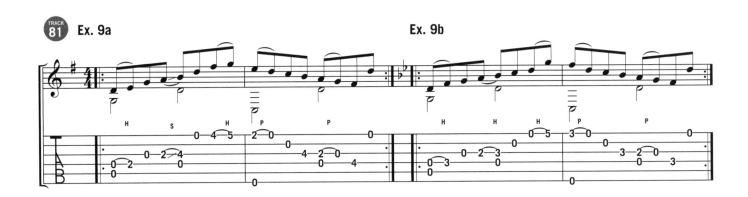

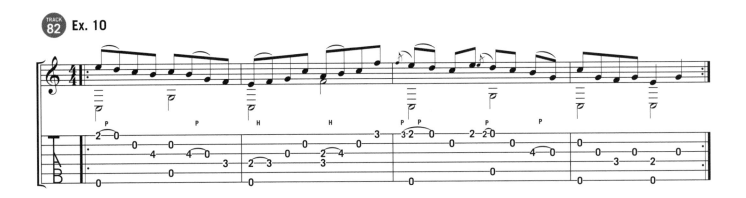

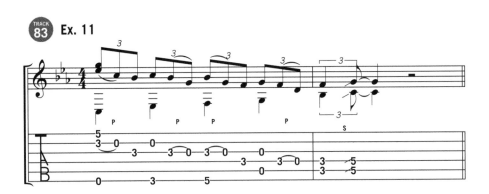

possible to easily switch between major and minor tonality, as seen in **Example 12**. Simply flat the E and B notes for a melancholy, minor sound like the one in Example 9b.

The key of D isn't quite as useful for playing leads as G and C—while all of the open strings work well in G and C, the C string is the flat seventh of D, making it more difficult to play major-key melodies. However, it remains a good key for accompaniment, and there's no reason why you can't throw in a riff here or there. **Examples 13 and 14** show a couple of D riffs—the first is sweet and the second is a little bluesy.

With these chords and riffs at your fingertips you can begin to explore uncharted regions of your musical potential. Remember, start by learning some quick chord changes and applying them to a song you know well, then let the fun begin. For more practice, check out the excerpt from my original song **"The Almost Whisky Waltz"** (the title track of a CD available through CD Baby). The song is in the key of C and offers you a chance to do some cross-picking and play all over the neck.

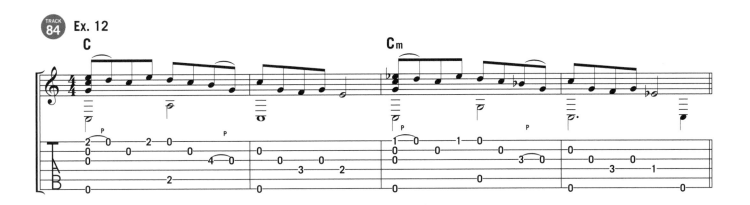

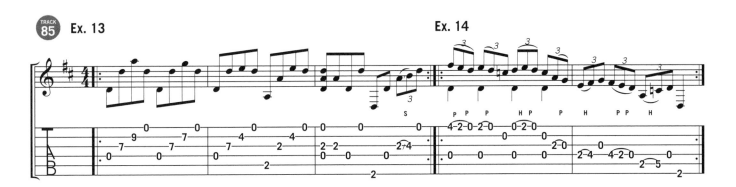

The Capo Is Your Friend

Unlike many altered tunings, Orkney allows you to play in more than one key without a capo, but what do you do for keys other than G, C, or D? The process is simple. Since C is four half steps below E, one easy way to play in E is to put your capo at the fourth fret (one fret for every half step) and play chord shapes for the key of C. You can think and act as though you're in C, but the sound coming out of your guitar will be in the key of E. Likewise, you can also play in E using your key-of-G chord shapes by moving the capo to the seventh fret, or your key-of-D chords with the capo at the second fret.

Each of these three positions (C, G, and D) yields its own unique textural and melodic possibilities. For any given key, try moving the capo around and see what each position has to offer!

The Almost Whisky Waltz

Music by Steve Baughman

Played up to Speed

Orkney tuning: C G D G C D

HIGH-STRUNG TUNING

Doug Young

For many people, playing a guitar in a foreign tuning can be an intimidating experience. Not so for high-strung tuning, often called Nashville tuning. High-strung tuning is similar to standard tuning—you can use all the same chord shapes—but the bottom four strings of the guitar are raised an octave; the third string is actually tuned higher than the first! You can use any guitar for Nashville tuning, but don't try this with standard-gauge strings. One way to find appropriate strings is to cannibalize a 12-string set, using just the lighter-gauge string from each pair (note that the first and second strings are the same gauge in most 12-string sets). Some string manufacturers also produce sets of strings for this very purpose, such as D'Addario's EJ38H set, which features lighter-gauge replacements for the bottom four strings.

In spite of the name, high-strung tuning has been used for more than just the "Nashville sound." The Rolling Stones used it frequently (in particular, on their hit "Wild Horses"). Other examples include Pink Floyd's "Hey You" and Kansas's "Dust in the Wind," both of which feature a prominent high-strung guitar. In this lesson, we'll explore the sonic and practical possibilities of this tuning, which helps get some extra mileage out of what you already know.

Double a Guitar in Standard Tuning

Once you've changed all those strings, you'll discover a marvelously bright and distinctive sound that may just change the way you look at the guitar. High-strung tuning is typically used for rhythm guitar, often doubling a normal guitar. Mark Casstevens, a veteran Nashville studio guitarist with hundreds of hit records to his credit, explains, "Sometimes when I don't want to use a 12-string, I will overdub the exact same part using a high-strung guitar. It doesn't have the same timbre as a 12-string, but it's another way to get the same effect."

The simple four-chord rhythm pattern in **Example 1** can be played on a normal guitar but takes on a completely different texture when played on a high-strung guitar. Notice the cool sound of the high C♯ on the third string against the doubled E on the first and second strings. Invite a friend to play along in standard tuning, or record two guitars on different tracks to hear the effect. Aside from its interesting sound, a high-strung guitar also offers some practical advantages when playing with others. "I've used it to stay out of the piano's range, because the guitar can get kind of thick on certain kinds of rhythms," Casstevens says.

TRACK 87 Tuning: E A D G B E

TRACK 88 Ex. 1

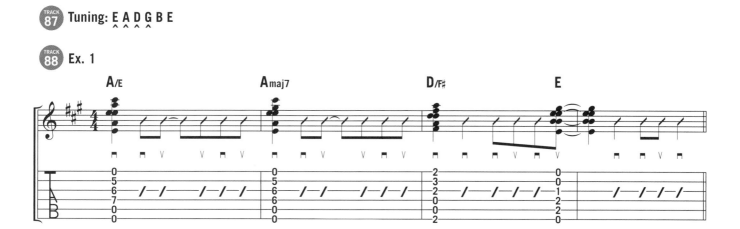

High-strung tuning also works well with fingerpicking patterns. **Example 2** is a high-strung fingerpicked pattern over the chord progression from Example 1. You can even combine the two examples—another guitarist can play the strumming pattern in Example 1 on a standard-tuned guitar while you fingerpick Example 2 on a high-strung guitar. Fingerpicking the same pattern on two guitars—one tuned to standard and the other strung high—can also yield some interesting results. The technique has been used effectively on many recordings, including the Judds' "Mama He's Crazy," in which Casstevens and fellow Nashville guitarist Don Potter play the same fingerpicking roll, an octave apart. Enlist a friend with a standard-tuned guitar so you can both finger-pick **Example 3**, with two guitars in octaves.

High-Strung Origins

Although no one is sure who invented Nashville tuning, one story is that Nashville A-Team session player Ray Edenton stumbled onto the tuning in the 1950s, when he broke his third string during a session and the only available replacement was a lighter-gauge banjo string. (However, Edenton himself recalls, "I used to do a lot of sessions with Chet Atkins, and I believe he came up with it on electric guitar. I put it on acoustic. Then Grady Martin handed me a guitar one day and it had four high strings on it!") This high-G tuning became a signature sound for Edenton; he and other Nashville players have used high-strung tunings on countless hits ever since.

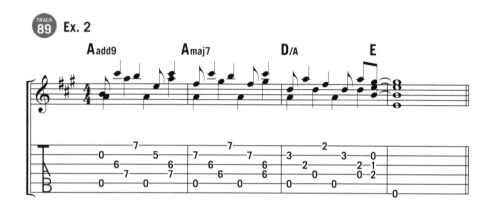

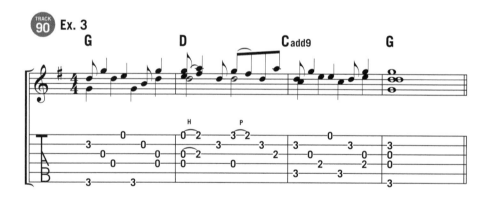

Play Old Licks in a Whole New Way

A high-strung guitar can sometimes magically transform tunes and licks you already know. **Example 4** is a fairly typical flatpicked strumming pattern with a bass line that connects the chords. Playing this example on a high-strung guitar moves the bass part up an octave, converting it to a melodic line.

High-strung tuning doesn't have to be restricted to accompaniment. Hearing another guitarist play Tarrega's "Etude in E minor" on a high-strung guitar inspired me to try the 16th-century pavan "The Earle of Salisbury" (**Example 5**)—a stately piece that has been recorded by John Renbourn. The high strings move the countermelody to a different register, giving the piece a lute-like sound.

You can also arrange tunes specifically to take advantage of the high-strung sound. Try out my fingerstyle arrangement of the English folk tune **"John Barleycorn"** on page 60. This arrangement places the melody on the higher-sounding middle strings and uses the top two strings primarily as drones.

As with the pavan, the result is a delicate sound with a unique texture. Although this arrangement works well as a high-strung solo-guitar piece, you can also experiment with the techniques used in earlier examples. A second guitarist could double the tune on a standard-tuned guitar or play chord accompaniment to fill in the low end.

Experiment with Familiar Techniques

What else can you do with this tuning? Just about anything. Rock power chords are very cool. High-strung versions of D A D G A D, open-D, or open-G tunings sound fantastic. Other variations abound, as well. Some players raise just the bottom three strings. Pat Metheny used a baritone guitar with the middle two strings up an octave on his CD *One Quiet Night*, while San Francisco guitarist Steve Baughman sometimes tunes his fifth string up an octave. You can play high-pitched lead guitar in first position. But watch out—you may find yourself wishing for another guitar so you can always keep one high-strung!

TRACK 91 Ex. 4

TRACK 92 Ex. 5

John Barleycorn

Traditional, arranged by Doug Young

 Played up to Speed

Tuning: E A D G B E

Verse

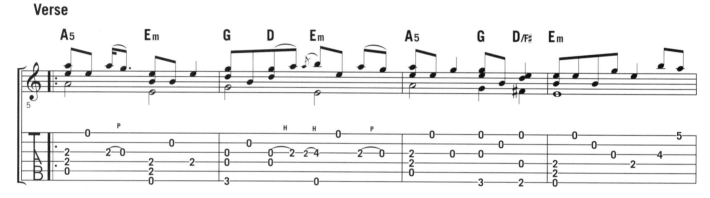

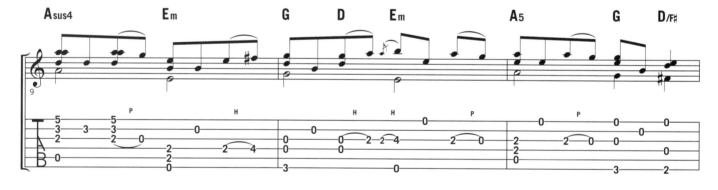

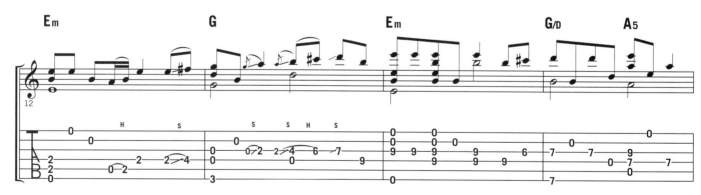

PRELUDE FROM THE CELLO SUITE NO. 1 IN G MAJOR

Music by Johann Sebastian Bach, arranged by Patrick Francis

The music of Johann Sebastian Bach has been widely transcribed for classical guitar, including a vast array of pieces originally written for solo cello, solo violin, lute, and keyboard. Over the years, Bach's suites for solo cello have been a favorite source of material for transcribers, not only because of Bach's compositional genius and the suites' beauty, but also because the works transfer relatively easily to the guitar. Such is the case with the Prelude from the Cello Suite No. 1 in G major, transcribed here and found on plenty of recorded interpretations by great classical players like Andrés Segovia and John Williams.

Bach's brilliance, mastery of counterpoint, and single-line writing are highlighted in his solo string works, where a single line may imply two or three voices. The sparseness of this single-line texture invites guitarists to add bass notes, displace octaves in the bass line, and "fill in" chords. In this arrangement, the Prelude is transposed from the original key of G major to D major, using dropped-D tuning. I've tried to strike a balance between adhering to the original score and adapting the work as a transcription for solo guitar.

In the original version, Bach made frequent use of the cello's resonant open strings, which often appear as pedal tones. On the guitar, dropped-D tuning affords guitarists a similar luxury of employing the open fifth and sixth strings. Some players choose to phrase the measures with repeated figures (like those in measures 1 through 8) with an echo effect, making the first two beats loud, followed by a quieter dynamic on beats three and four. At measure 31, the melody moves into the lower voice. Here, playing the low notes with the thumb will really bring out the moving line until the texture changes at measure 37. Finally, to end with a bang, crescendo over measures 37 and 38 and maintain the dynamic intensity until the end of the piece, culminating at the final chord, strummed loudly. To make the ending more compelling, try a slight ritard on the final beat of measure 41.

—*Patrick Francis*

TRACK 94 **Dropped-D Tuning: D A D G B E**

TRACK 95 **Played up to Speed**

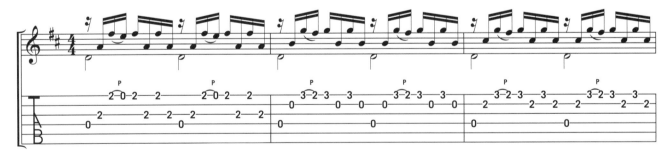

EXPLORE ALTERNATE TUNINGS

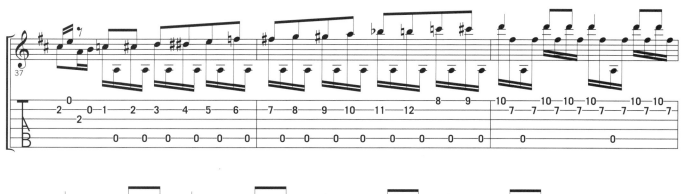

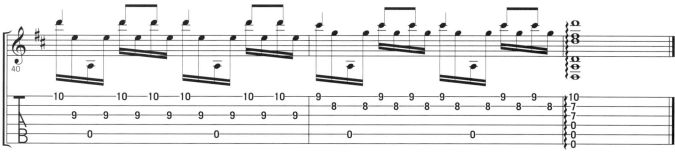

OLD JOE CLARK

Traditional, arranged by Joe Miller

One of America's best-known fiddle tunes, "Old Joe Clark" has been recorded by Doc Watson, Pete Seeger, Bill Monroe, and many others. Early recordings by Fiddlin' Powers and the Skillet Lickers were big country hits in the 1920s. Although there are conflicting stories about where the tune was written, there is a historical marker in Sextons Creek, Kentucky, where Old Joe Clark is supposed to have once lived. In part, it reads: "Joe Clark, born 1839, lived here; a shiftless and rough mountaineer of that day. His enemies were legion; he was murdered in 1885."

This arrangement is played harp-style, in which the melody constantly moves from one string to another. If you are careful to let each string ring for as long as possible, a beautiful legato effect can be achieved. The picking-hand patterns may seem awkward at first, but they are quite comfortable once you get used to them. The important thing is to avoid using the same finger of the picking hand twice in a row.

In measures 6, 10, and 18, feel free to substitute your own licks where there are pauses in the melody. Use a capo on the second fret to play in the key of A (the key that fiddlers usually use for this tune), or higher up the neck to make the fretting-hand stretches easier.

—Joe Miller

TRACK 96 Tuning: D G D G B E

TRACK 97 Played up to Speed

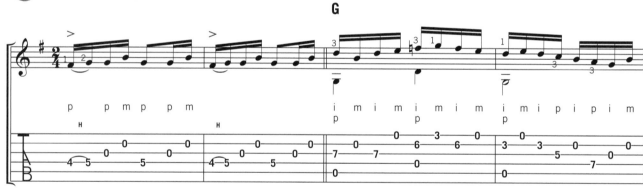

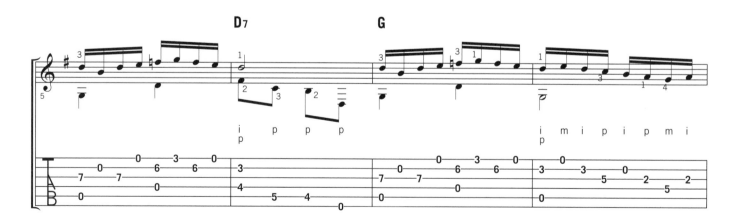

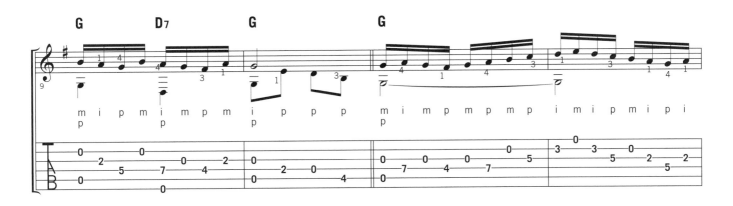

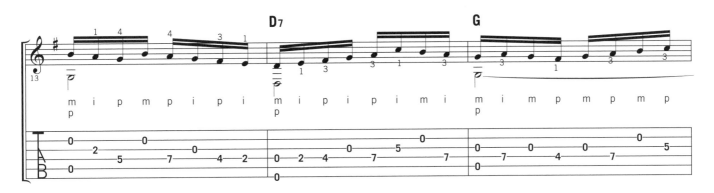

HI'ILAWE

Music by Sam Li'a Kalainaina, Sr., arranged by Patrick Landeza

f *ki ho'alu*—the Hawaiian slack-key guitar tradition—had a national anthem, it would be "Hi'ilawe." Composed in the late 19th century, by Sam Li'a Kalainaina, Sr., the song's title refers to the twin waterfalls located in Waipio Valley on the Big Island of Hawaii and is considered a staple of any slack-key repertoire. The late, great Gabby "Pops" Pahinui recorded "Hi'ilawe" with his sons in 1972 and made it famous. Pahinui may not have invented slack-key guitar, but he is responsible for inspiring many of us who play within the genre today.

You'll notice this song is in a dropped-C tuning (C G D G B D), which gives the song a very rich low-C bass note on the sixth string. As for tempo, the song takes on a different life with each player and situation. Even Pahinui tailored his tempo to his circumstances—on his solo recordings, he played it fairly slow (around 70 bpm), but picked up the tempo somewhat when playing with a band (around 90 bpm). The song's main melodic figure (heard in measure 1 and repeated throughout the song) should evoke the steady flow of the twin waterfalls that give the song its name. Use your index finger to hammer onto the C note on the second string, and you should be in the perfect position to play the other notes of the C chord that kicks off the following measure (if you're unfamiliar with a C-chord shape in dropped-C tuning, the entire chord is shown in the song's final measure). The song's A section uses only two chords, C and G7 (the I and V7 chords in the key of C). When you get to the song's B section at measure 11, the harmony also includes an F chord (the IV of C), which bears a strong resemblance to the F chord from standard tuning. Have fun with it, and don't forget to play with the spirit of aloha.

—*Patrick Landeza*

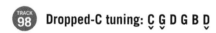

Dropped-C tuning: C G D G B D

Played up to Speed

ABOUT THE TEACHERS

Steve Baughman

Steve Baughman is a San Francisco guitarist who loves guitar music with melody, especially Celtic and Appalachian music. His CDs include *Life in Prism, The Almost Whisky Waltz*, and *A Drop of the Pure*, on his own Tall Trees label (celticguitar.com), and he appears with Pierre Bensusan, Martin Simpson, and others on the Rounder Records compilation *Ramble to Cashel*. Baughman is also author of the Mel Bay books *Celtic Guitar Method* and *Celtic Fingerstyle Solos*. He is a partner in the San Francisco law firm of Baughman and Wang, where he practices primarily in the area of political asylum law.

Patrick Francis

Patrick Francis (francisguitar.com) picked up a guitar at age 12 and immersed himself in the study of various musical styles, eventually earning a doctor of musical arts degree in classical guitar in 1996. Patrick composes and arranges for solo guitar as well as guitar ensemble, and he currently directs the classical guitar program at San Jose State University. He has toured nationally and internationally and his original music can be heard on the disc *Verdes Años*, recorded by his guitar and clarinet duo *Azulão* (cdbaby.com/cd/azulao).

Fran Guidry

Fran Guidry (kaleponi.com) fell in love with *ki ho‘alu*—Hawaiian slack-key guitar—the first time he heard it in a Waikiki hotel room in 1999. Since then he has studied and performed with some of today's foremost slack-key guitarists, including Patrick Landeza, Dennis Kamakahi, Cyril Pahinui, and Ledward Kaapana. Fran released his first CD, *Kaleponi*, in 2007. He performs in the San Francisco Bay Area as a solo artist and as a member of Kawili, a Hawaiian string band. Veteran slack-key artist Kevin Brown of Maui says of Fran, "His slack-key playing is straight from the heart, and that is the key that unlocks this soulful music we know as *ki ho‘alu*."

Mark Hanson

Mark Hanson has authored more than 30 titles on guitar, including three on alternate tunings. As a fingerstyle guitarist, Hanson won a Grammy in 2005 for his contributions to *Henry Mancini: Pink Guitar*, and his D A D G A D instrumental "Drake's Passage" aired on *American Idol*. Each summer Hanson hosts the Accent on Music Guitar Seminar in Portland, Oregon; details at accentonmusic.com. In an earlier life as an editor at *Frets* magazine, he interviewed such luminaries as James Taylor, David Crosby, and Larry Carlton.

David Hodge

David Hodge has for years provided backup to numerous Berkshire County, Massachusetts, singer-songwriters. But teaching music is his first love; in addition to his private students, he teaches group guitar lessons for the Berkshire Community College. And guitar students of all ages and levels from more than 168 countries read his lessons at Guitar Noise (guitar-noise.com). He is the author of *The Complete Idiot's Guide to Playing Bass Guitar* (Alpha Books).

Patrick Landeza

Award-winning musician, songwriter, producer, and educator Patrick Landeza (patricklandeza. com) is considered to be a leading force behind Hawaiian slack-key guitar, or *ki ho'alu*, on the mainland. Born and raised to Hawaiian parents on the island of Berkeley, California, Landeza remains mindful of the lessons he learned as a teen from his renowned mentors: Raymond Kane, Cyril Pahinui, George Kuo, and Dennis Kamakahi. Patrick is the founder of the Institute of Hawaiian Music and Culture and contributes to *Acoustic Guitar* magazine as well as other publications. He has three albums under his belt along with a successful slack-key instructional DVD *Slack Key Made Easy* (Lamb Productions) and a slack-key play-along called *Slack Tracks*. Currently, Landeza tours and conducts slack-key workshops around the country with his musical friends.

Sean McGowan

Sean McGowan (maplesugarmusic.com) is a fingerstyle jazz and acoustic guitarist who combines diverse influences with unconventional techniques to create a broad palette of textures within his compositions and arrangements for solo guitar. His first recording, *River Coffee*, was featured on BBC radio, and he's had music published in Mel Bay's *Master Anthology of Fingerstyle Guitar, Vol. 3*. His recording *Indigo* is a collection of jazz standards and originals for solo archtop guitar. A regular contributor to *Acoustic Guitar* magazine, McGowan teaches guitar, theory, and improvisation at the University of Colorado–Denver.

Joe Miller

Joe Miller has performed at acoustic music festivals across the U.S. and Canada. He has studied with about 35 music teachers, including classical guitarist Bill Trotter in Toronto and sitarist Nikhil Banerjee. A past winner of both the California State Flatpicking Championship and the National Fingerpicking Championship, he has released 2 CDs of instrumental music, available on iTunes and at CD Baby. He teaches at Eric Schoenberg Guitars in Tiburon, California.

Jeffrey Pepper Rodgers

Jeffrey Pepper Rodgers (jeffreypepperrodgers.com) is the founding editor of *Acoustic Guitar* magazine and author of *Teach Yourself Guitar Basics*, *The Complete Singer-Songwriter*, and the interview collection *Rock Troubadours*. Rodgers' song "Fly," from the solo CD *Humming My Way Back Home*, won a grand prize in the John Lennon Songwriting Contest. In 2010 Rodgers released *Dead to the Core*, featuring his solo acoustic arrangements of Grateful Dead songs, and a companion video called *Learn Seven Grateful Dead Classics for Acoustic Guitar* (Homespun). He lives outside Syracuse, New York, where he writes and edits for *Acoustic Guitar*, reports on the music scene for NPR's *All Things Considered*, and teaches workshops and university courses on songwriting, guitar, and nonfiction writing.

Doug Young

Doug Young lives and performs in the San Francisco Bay Area. He is a frequent contributor to *Acoustic Guitar* and has had the pleasure of interviewing many of his heroes, from Pierre Bensusan to Tommy Emmanuel. When Young's not working on new guitar pieces, he's usually recording himself or others in his home studio, where he recorded his self-produced CD, *Laurel Mill* (dougyoungguitar.com). Young's instructional book *Understanding DADGAD for Fingerstyle Guitar* was published by Mel Bay.

More Titles from Stringletter

 **The Acoustic Guitar Method Complete Edition**
Book and 3 CDs
136 pp., $24.99
HL00695667

 **The Acoustic Guitar Fingerstyle Method**
Book and 2 CDs
80 pp., $24.99
HL00331948

 **The Acoustic Guitar Method Chord Book**
Book
48 pp., $15.99
HL00695722

 **Rhythm Guitar Essentials**
Book and CD
71 pp., $19.99
HL00696062

 **Bluegrass Guitar Essentials**
Book and CD
72 pp., $19.99
HL00695931

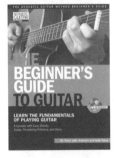 **The Beginner's Guide to Guitar**
Book and CD
66 pp., $19.99
HL00696461

 **Flatpicking Guitar Essentials**
Book and CD
96 pp., $19.99
HL00699174

 **Fingerstyle Guitar Essentials**
Book and CD
88 pp., $19.99
HL00699145

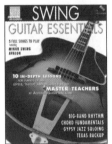 **Swing Guitar Essentials**
Book and CD
80 pp., $19.99
HL00699193

 **Roots and Blues Fingerstyle Guitar**
Book and CD
96 pp., $19.99
HL00699214

 **Alternate Tunings Guitar Essentials**
Book and CD
96 pp., $19.99
HL00695557

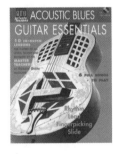 **Acoustic Blues Guitar Essentials**
Book and CD
72 pp., $19.99
HL00699186

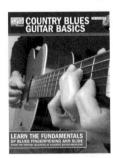 **Country Blues Guitar Basics**
Book and CD
64 pp., $19.99
HL00696222

 **Acoustic Guitar Accompaniment Basics**
Book and CD
64 pp., $14.99
HL00695430

 **Acoustic Guitar Solo Fingerstyle Basics**
Book and CD
64 pp., $14.99
HL00695597

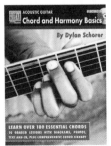 **Acoustic Guitar Chord and Harmony Basics**
Book and CD
72 pp., $16.99
HL00695611

 **Acoustic Guitar Slide Basics**
Book and CD
72 pp., $16.99
HL00695610

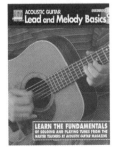 **Acoustic Guitar Lead and Melody Basics**
Book and CD
64 pp., $14.99
HL00695492

FOR MORE INFORMATION, SEE YOUR LOCAL MUSIC DEALER OR WRITE TO:
EXCLUSIVELY DISTRIBUTED BY

 HAL•LEONARD®

7777 W. BLUEMOUND RD. P.O. BOX 13819 MILWAUKEE, WI 53213
VISIT HAL LEONARD ONLINE AT WWW.HALLEONARD.COM